USING
MASS
COMMUNICATION
THEORY

USING MASS COMMUNICATION THEORY

Maxwell E. McCombs

Syracuse University

Lee B. Becker

Ohio State University

Prentice-Hall, Inc., Englewood Cliffs, New Jersey 07632

Library of Congress Cataloging in Publication Data

McCombs, Maxwell E.
   Using mass communication theory.

   (Perspectives in mass communication)
   Bibliography: p.
   Includes index.
   1. Journalism. 2. Communication. I. Becker,
Lee B. (date) joint author. II. Title.
III. Series.
PN4731.M24   070.4'3   78-9893
ISBN 0-13-939702-7

PRENTICE-HALL PERSPECTIVES IN MASS COMMUNICATION SERIES
edited by John L. Hulteng and Edward J. Trayes

Printed in the United States of America

10 9 8 7 6 5 4 3 2 1

Editorial/production supervision by Lynda Heideman
Cover design by Hernandez-Porto
Manufacturing buyer: Trudy Pisciotti

6949

PRENTICE-HALL INTERNATIONAL, INC., *London*
PRENTICE-HALL OF AUSTRALIA PTY. LIMITED, *Sydney*
PRENTICE-HALL OF CANADA, LTD., *Toronto*
PRENTICE-HALL OF INDIA PRIVATE LIMITED, *New Delhi*
PRENTICE-HALL OF JAPAN, INC., *Tokyo*
PRENTICE-HALL OF SOUTHEAST ASIA PTE. LTD., *Singapore*
WHITEHALL BOOKS LIMITED, *Wellington, New Zealand*

Contents

PART THREE
THE COMMUNITY *99*

CONCLUSION *129*

Series Editors' Note

The Perspectives in Mass Communication series offers great flexibility to instructors and students in courses in communication or the mass media and society area. Each volume in the series deals with a specific aspect of mass communication, and each is authored by scholars chosen for their competence to develop that topic intensively and authoritatively.

Among the volumes included in this series is one that inventories the media fields today and traces historical and developmental patterns. Another identifies and analyzes the forces and motivations that influence the functioning of contemporary news media. One volume views the media as expressions of popular culture and examines their significance in that role. Others explore a range of relevant topics, including the theories of mass communication and the interrelationship between the advertising industry and the media.

This modular approach allows for combining two, three, or more of the compact volumes in the series into a composite text, permitting the instructor to tailor the text materials to the emphases desired in a particular course or to the needs of a particular group of students. An individual title may also be used as the core text for an introductory course on its topic.

Taken as a whole, the series provides a comprehensive, multi-dimensional understanding of the media of mass communication, particularly those media devoted either primarily or in part to the dissemination of news, information, and opinion.

JOHN L. HULTENG
EDWARD J. TRAYES

Preface

Students in most journalism programs learn a great deal about writing and something about reporting. They learn, in short, about message production. But they don't learn much about what happens to a message once it is produced. They don't learn about the various influences that shape the information gathering and message production phase of their work. And they don't learn enough about the social context of the communication process.

Because there is much more to journalism than message production, this book provides an overview of our factual knowledge about the interaction of mass communications and society. This overview is not based on conjecture or idiosyncratic personal experience, but on the empirical investigations of mass communications conducted by social scientists from a variety of disciplines.

We have tried to organize that empirical research from the point of view of the practicing journalist, to make it most useful to the journalism student. In a real sense, we've tried to do more than merely review the literature. Our presentation of existing literature and distillation of implications forms the basis of what social scientists call theory.

Theory is a map. It is based on observations from the past, but it is geared toward the future. It helps to explain. And it helps to predict. There is nothing so practical as a good theory, social scientist Kurt Levin once remarked, for theory helps us deal with the world around us.

Journalistic theory should help reporters and editors anticipate audience reactions to their copy. It should help them understand better the newsgathering process. And it should help them understand the context of the mass communication process in which they work.

Others may prefer to organize the literature in a way different from the one we have chosen. To be sure, newer and perhaps clearer examples of some of our points may come along. But we have provided at least one framework here, and it will, we feel confident, be of value to future journalists.

In presenting this literature for journalists to use, we've discussed what some may call the "classics"—major studies, some from several decades ago, that have shaped the field of communications. Their findings, in other words, have determined to a large degree what kind of research followed, and what we know today.

We've also used recent examples of research, small pieces of data where they help tell the story, and, where appropriate, anecdotes. In each case, we've presented the materials simply, and no prior knowledge of research is assumed. This book is thus an entry point for the student who is aware that journalism is more than message production.

Persons interested in pursuing any of the topics we've discussed may turn to the materials cited in the bibliography at the end of the book. Rather than encumber the text with extensive footnotes, we have assembled key materials in the bibliography, divided according to appropriate section in the text. Readers should have few problems finding additional details on studies cited or further readings in areas of particular interest to them.

The production of this text has been a learning experience for us. It forced us to view communication research and communication theory from our former vantage point as working journalists. It is our hope that it makes better journalists out of those reading the text.

USING
MASS
COMMUNICATION
THEORY

INTRODUCTION

1
Messages versus Communications

Among the images commonly evoked by mention of the mass media are printing presses with their flashing blur of newsprint, television studios with bat-
teries of cameras and lights, clattering wire service teletypewriters, and much
of the other technological paraphernalia that are part of the mass media of
communication. Asked to name the principal mass media, the typical person
responds: "Newspapers, radio, and television." Each of these media is based
on a distinctive technology that has been applied to the widespread distribution
of news, entertainment, and advertising.

If the images do not focus directly on the technologies that make possible
this widespread distribution of messages, they tend to focus on the plethora of
messages produced by these technologies. The term *mass communication*, often
used synonymously with *mass media*, directs our attention to the vast outpour-
ing of messages that is a prime characteristic of the mass communication
media. One visualizes stacks of freshly printed newspapers, and magazine
stands heaped with periodicals of every type and taste. One thinks of the end-
less succession of radio programs available in most urban areas and the ever
increasing number of television programs as cable supplements direct broadcasting.

Technology and messages—these are the visual images commonly
evoked by the phrases *mass media* and *mass communication*. In many ways,
these are unfortunate focal points for our thoughts about journalism and
mass communications because technology and messages are nothing more than
artifacts of the *communication process*. Neither the intricate and sophisticated

technologies on which mass communication is based nor the vast outpourings of messages these technologies enable us to produce are the communication process itself.

As journalists we are professional observers and communicators of the day's news. All the technology we use is nothing more than a set of tools. All the messages we produce are simply by-products (written, recorded, or video-taped) of what we hope has been a successful effort in telling others, many others, what is the news of the day.

Ironically, when we think about, or describe, two people talking with each other, the focus is on two persons interacting. The view is a *behavioral* one focused on human activities, not on the medium of communication or on the literal messages produced. Perhaps this is because no machinery—no invented technology—is interposed between the two people involved in interpersonal communication.

But when we shift from the simplest form of communication—two people engaged in a thoughtful conversation—to the more complex forms of mass communication, somehow our attention is distracted. We focus on the technologies interposed between the sender and the receiver and the sudden multiplication in the volume of messages dispatched. These unfortunate distractions divert our attention from essential elements of the communication process. While technology and multiple messages are necessary elements in mass communication, they are far from sufficient for any actual *communication* to take place.

A TECHNOLOGICAL PROCESS

Mass communication involves, but is far more than, a technological process that multiplies the *range* and *penetration* of a sender's message. Technology first changed human communication by extending its geographic range. Postal service enabled persons quite remote from each other to exchange messages. With the telegraph, the press for the first time was able effectively to cover the entire nation and even the world, and the speed of exchanging messages was greatly increased. Similarly, the appearance of broadcasting, first radio in the 1920s and then television in the 1940s, further extended the range of spoken and audio-visual messages. Cable now has entered the mass communication marketplace to extend further the range and scope of audio-visual communication.

Technology also enables senders to duplicate their messages many fold or to deliver them simultaneously to many recipients. The emergence in the 1830s of the penny press, the first of the mass media, was dependent on the availability of printing technology that could produce a large number of copies rapidly. With the penny press, newspaper circulation began to be measured in the thousands, and a substantial proportion of the households in each city was reached by newspapers.

A century later the pentration of radio was so complete in the United States that a person could walk down the street of most American neighborhoods on Sunday evening and hear, quite continuously, that week's version of Jack Benny, Edgar Bergen and Charlie McCarthy, or the other radio favorites of that era.

These two phenomena, wide geographic range and high penetration among the population, have intrigued observers of mass communication. They also have made some people apprehensive about the social impact and power of these seemingly ubiquitous sources of communication. But to describe the tremendous range and penetration of mass communication, to focus on its masterful technologies and its plethora of messages, says nothing about the effectiveness of this communication process, which is both a *technological process* and a *behavioral process*.

Our images of mass media and mass communication may center on technology and messages, but this view ignores whether any actual communication has taken place. The successful distribution of messages is only the first step toward effective communication. Successful communication implies that the message has been received and understood as well as produced and distributed.

A BEHAVIORAL PROCESS

Communication is a process involving some very complex human behaviors by both the sender and the receiver of each message. To understand communication and to communicate effectively, each journalist must thoroughly grasp the principle that production of a message does not equal communication. Simply to produce and disseminate a message, no matter how eloquent its language, its style, and its content, is not communication. No matter how sophisticated our technology and how efficient our distribution systems, there is no guaranteed audience for any message that the journalist, or any other mass communicator, produces. And even receipt of the message does not guarantee that it will be understood.

A recent scientific survey in an East Coast city illustrates this point. This survey found that less than one-third of the men and women who picked up the newspaper the day they were interviewed even noticed the *typical* news item. And less than 20 percent actually read the headline plus some portion of the text. Only about 15 percent read *most* of the average news item. While stories placed on the front page received a much higher level of notice—about half the audience noticed those stories—even those prominently displayed items ended up with no more than 15 percent of the audience reading most of the story.

Another survey of readers in a northeastern urban area with a morning and an evening newspaper found that only seven columns and features in the two newspapers were read regularly by as much as half the newspaper audience. The seven features were out of the one hundred regularly appearing in those newspapers. It is not an atypical finding. And, of course, no newspaper reaches every household in its city. Some people simply are not convinced that there are interesting or useful messages for them in the daily newspaper.

A similar situation exists in broadcasting. Messages pour into the air, but is anyone listening? The national audience survey of the A. C. Nielsen Company shows that even during the prime evening hours less than half of the American population usually are viewing television. The peak viewing time is nine o'clock, but even at the peak only among children age six to eleven, adult women, and men over age fifty are a majority of the people viewing television. And even at that hour it is a bare majority.

There simply is no guaranteed audience for your message, regardless of when it is delivered, how sophisticated the technology used to deliver it, or the amount of creativity used to produce it. Production of a message is just one part of the communication process, and unless this message production is attuned to the full communication process, your message may not gain any audience at all.

FEEDBACK

A paradoxical question is, If a tree falls unobserved in the forest, does it make a sound? In the case of unobserved messages, there is no paradox at all. An unobserved message does not communicate. It is wasted effort. Because unobserved messages—all those unread newspaper articles, all those unwatched television shows—do not communicate anything, *feedback* is a very practical concern of the mass media.

When you talk with another person you receive instantaneous feedback: your message usually is followed directly by the person's verbal reply. Even while you are delivering the message you receive nonverbal feedback in the form of facial expressions, gestures, and other physical movements. But in mass communication the audience is remote and unseen by the communicator, and a direct reply rarely occurs. There is the occasional telephone call or letter, and there are indirect forms of long-term feedback like subscription cancellations, but these provide very little feedback for the day-to-day work of journalists and their editors.

So each of the mass media has devised techniques for obtaining more detailed and more direct feedback from its audience. Newspapers and magazines often conduct *readership surveys* in which scientific samples of their audiences are shown copies of the newspaper or magazine and asked to indicate which articles they actually read. Other surveys probe audiences' attitudes, their lifestyles, and the uses they make of mass communication. These surveys seek to understand and explain the differences between readers and nonreaders, between frequent and infrequent readers, and between readers of competing publications.

In broadcasting, the suppliers of feedback information are major satellites of the radio and television industry. Nielsen and Arbitron provide the program ratings that determine television programming schedules. Through meters attached to TV sets indicating when the sets are turned on and what channel they are tuned to, through diaries filled out by members of randomly selected households describing what programs they have viewed each week, through telephone surveys asking what program the respondent is viewing at the moment, and through personal interviews covering attitudes, lifestyles, uses of television, and program preferences, the networks and individual television and radio stations receive extensive data on the audiences for their programs.

For newspapers, magazines, and television, the volume of available feedback data on *advertising messages* is especially large. For the commercial enterprise investing part of its income in advertising, and for the commercial mass media that largely support themselves by marketing their audiences to advertisers, hard evidence on the size of the audience and hard information describing that audience's attitudes and interests are well worth the substantial amounts of money spent on planned feedback. Advertisers, perhaps better than any other group of mass communicators, are well aware that no audience is guaranteed for any message, no matter how sophisticated the technology and how clever the message. To communicate with its intended audience each message must be attuned carefully to that audience.

More sophisticated forms of planned feedback go well beyond establishing the simple existence of an audience for the message. They also consider an audience's interest in the message, its understanding of the message content, its ability to respond meaningfully to the message, and sometimes its acceptance of the message. Going beyond simple evidence of effective distribution is important: putting the newspaper on the doorstep and attracting a family to tune in your TV program each week is the first step toward effective communication, but it is only the first step.

Some years ago when "I Love Lucy" was America's number one television show, it was dropped by its sponsor, a major manufacturer of cigarettes. All the evidence clearly indicated the popularity of this show, which drew millions of viewers each week. Why was it dropped? Because, while the feedback indicated a huge audience, it also revealed that few heavy smokers were in that audience. For an advertiser with messages touting cigarettes, this highly popular show was a poor vehicle for communication.

BARRIERS TO COMMUNICATION

Since reception of a message is essential to communication, the journalist must overcome the barriers to, and optimize reception of, the message. Of course, the barriers to reception are not the only barriers to successful communication. As we've noted earlier, communication assumes understanding. Journalists cannot be satisfied with merely knowing that their stories have been read or viewed or listened to. If the journalist wants to communicate something, he or she wants the audience members to *understand* what the story is all about.

The barriers to *understanding,* however, further complicate the process of communication. Audience members have the ability to misperceive messages and can distort the message in various ways. In other words, what they understand can be quite different from what the message was designed to tell them.

In a sense, the journalist isn't concerned with audience understanding of the message *per se.* The journalist wants the audience members to understand the *objective reality* on which the story is based. Successful communication for the journalist involves audience understanding of the real world about them. For any given message, successful communication involves an understanding of the actual phenomenon on which that story is based.

Barriers to *message construction* also endanger successful communication. The journalist is hampered in newsgathering by myriad factors. Sources may not provide information. Physical and temporal restraints may keep the reporter from gathering all essential information. The result is impaired message construction—and disrupted communication.

Some barriers and constraints on communication, especially those imposed by the audience, can be made explicit through planned feedback. Well-designed research projects can reveal an audience's language patterns, attitudes and interests, perceptual habits, and the nexus of interpersonal relationships that impinge on the success of any message. But since new research cannot be carried out for every new message, workaday knowledge by the journalist of these barriers to successful communication means having some knowledge of *communication theory* and the many variables that ultimately determine the outcome of each communication endeavor. Communication theory also includes characteristics of the communicator and mass media organizations that influence the ultimate outcome of the communication process, and knowledge of this theory can help journalists understand the barriers to effective communication.

Too often, journalism students—and their professors who design the courses and the curriculum—concentrate heavily on message production. Courses in news *writing* and *editing* dominate the professional education of many students. The origins of this concentration are understandable. Journalism is a major professional outlet for students who enjoy writing. This focus on writing is perpetuated by the practices of the newsroom, and one myth of

American journalism is that every newsroom harbors at least one author of *the* great American novel. In most news organizations, as well, writing and editing are the dominant tasks. The official designation for the position of reporter in many organizations is "staff writer."

Students and journalists are thus led to view their job in terms of writing and message production. In the newsroom bureaucracy, the journalist's job is message production, with secondary emphasis on gathering news and originating new information. Concern over the mass communication process and the effectiveness of all those messages receive little explicit attention in the bureaucracy.

STYLEBOOKS

Because bureaucracies depend on routine procedures to achieve efficient operation, the stylebook is a key part of the message handling routine. All good journalism students and journalists learn the stylebook of their organization because it is essential knowledge for good performance as a message writer. But how many journalism students or journalists learn the details of a social psychology text or communication theory book with equal thoroughness? This knowledge should be just as routinely applied to message production as is knowledge of style. It is essential for effective communication.

These two elements—two notions of style, if you will—are brought together in speech communication's concern with rhetoric. Good rhetoric includes consistent style and perhaps even literary flourishes. But good rhetoric also is persuasive; it is effective communication that reaches and influences members of the audience. In recent years speech communication has thus turned to behavioral science for fuller scientific understanding of the psychology and sociology of the communication process.

Our concerns in journalism are similar, but not identical, to those of speech communication. Speech communication is concerned with interpersonal communication. Journalism is concerned with mass communication. And speech communicators are more concerned with persuasion than are journalists, who primarily seek to disseminate information. But a complete view of mass communication, and of message production for the mass media, combines style and effective communication.

Our task here is to produce a companion volume for use with the journalist's stylebook. Construction of effective messages requires knowledge of both style and human behavior. Journalism and all the mass communication professions depend on an understanding of human behavior to succeed in the real world. It is knowledge of human behavior and application of this knowledge to produce effective communications that distinguish the professional journalist from the technician.

The technician is only concerned that the message be produced in a stylistically satisfactory way and that it be disseminated as fully as possible. The professional journalist is concerned that the message actually be received and understood by members of the audience. The professional is interested in creating messages that reflect the real world. In other words, the professional is concerned with both the behaviors and techniques necessary for information transmittal and the behaviors and situations affecting how information is received by the public.

THEORIES OF COMMUNICATION

To repeat our central thesis: producing and distributing a message does not equal communication. For an overview of the message's place in the larger context of the mass communication process, consider Wilbur Schramm's model of communication, which contains three key elements—a sender, a message, and a receiver—plus feedback to make the process dynamic and ongoing. The message—on which students and journalists concentrate most of their attention—is only one of the three major elements that enter into the communication process. The Schramm model and others like it elaborate the many characteristics of the *sender* and *receiver* that influence the shape of the message and the outcome of the communication process. Because so many of these influential characteristics can significantly alter the intended outcome of the message, we have called these characteristics *barriers* to effective communication.

In this book, designed as a behavioral companion to the stylebook for message production, we will examine in some detail these barriers, these behavioral characteristics that impinge on the success of the communication. In other words, we will be presenting a *theory of communication* that *describes* the behavioral thicket into which each mass communication message is tossed. Unlike Brer Rabbit, few messages find the thicket a congenial environment. And, indeed, it is a thicket, as you will agree after seeing the number of barriers that lie in the way of successful communication.

Now a theory of communication, as the term is used here, does not mean some idealized, utopian picture of mass communication. The fact that we speak repeatedly of barriers to successful communication should eliminate any utopian connotations to our use of the term *theory*. Our theory is grounded in empirical observations of human behavior and mass communication—a realistic picture, not an idealized one.

Like a sketch or map of the real world, our theory does not reproduce every detail. Rather it outlines the salient features of that portion of the real world it pictures. Here the salient features are those factors that pose barriers to successful communication.

Our behavioral stylebook, our sketch of a theory of mass communication, will consider the marketplace where each news item competes for attention and understanding. Numerous barriers to successful communication exist in that marketplace. Each must be assessed in some detail so that message producers can explicitly take them into account.

In assessing these constraints on the communication process, we will begin with the message itself and examine how its contents relate to the intended audience's experience. It is obvious that communicator and audience must speak the same language if the message is to be understood. But it often is the case that people speaking a common language really do not share the same language. Lewis Carroll's poem ''Jabberwocky'' has the appearance and sound of English, but it does not communicate any meaning. In terms of the communication outcome, many mass media messages are the same gibberish. Chapter 2 discusses how language itself can be a major barrier.

Beyond the literal message, there is the question of how the message is perceived and understood by each member of the audience. Two witnesses to the same event, to the same mass communication, will not necessarily experience the same thing. *Perception* is a psychological as well as a mechanistic, physiological process. Individual differences are found in perception just as they are found in the understanding and retention of the message that follows. By the time we examine these barriers to effective communication in chapter 3 we are deeply into the consideration of how individual differences, the psychology of the individual in the audience, influence the communication process. Chapter 4 extends this psychological analysis to the patterns of exposure.

But individuals do not exist in isolation; they are part of a larger community and society and are members of many different groups. So in chapter 5 our catalog of the barriers to communication considers how individual behavior is modified by its social setting and how general social conditions affect audience behavior. An individual with little personal interest in politics often will follow the latest political news so he or she can participate in conversations with friends. People and their use of mass communication are influenced by their friends, family, and associates. Similarly, general social conditions—upcoming election, economic recession, cultural values and beliefs—also influence each individual's use of mass communication.

A complete theory of communication also must include the communicator, so we move in chapters 6 and 7 from the audience to the communicator who produces mass communication messages. This analysis parallels the analysis of the audience in many respects: just as the individual characteristics of audience members affect how a message is received and understood, the individual characteristics of personnel in the mass media also influence the shape of the message that is produced.

It is perhaps even more obvious for the communicator than it is for the audience that social setting has a significant impact on the mass communication process. After all, mass communications are produced by formal organiza ions, by bureaucracies of specialists who form the teams necessary to create and disseminate messages via the mass media. The characteristics of these organizational settings clearly constrain and influence the nature of the mass communication product.

And in turn, these mass communication organizations, like all formal organizations and institutions in our society, are constrained and influenced by the larger society in which they work. Chapter 8 focuses on the variety of legal, economic, cultural, and other social sanctions through which the community influences and constrains the performance of the mass media.

TWO SUMMARY THEMES

All these constraints and barriers to successful communication, affecting both the communicator and the audience, can be summarized in two themes. The first theme emphasizes the *progressive reduction* in content and behavior options that characterizes the flow of information from the real world to its ultimate destination, the individuals in the audience. The second theme emphasizes two *countervailing sets of influence,* the effects of the mass media on the audience *and* the effects of the audience, individually and collectively, on the mass media.

There are myriad stories in the world that could be communicated by the mass media. But there is a progressive winnowing as we move through the mass communication process. Legal sanctions make some information and material unavailable for mass communication. Economic constraints require choices about what will be noted and what will be ignored. There is a very real economic limit on how much the mass media can do. Only so many dollars are available. So extensive selection and discarding is necessary. The interests and mores of the community and audience served by a mass medium also dictate ignoring many topics of communication. And journalistic convention designates some events in the community as highly newsworthy and ignores many others.

Another principal task within each news organization is the winnowing and editing of the material available for dissemination. On a typical day, a local newspaper uses no more than 15 or 20 percent of all the material available in written reports. And as we have noted, much information is never even written up for perusal by the mass media gatekeepers.

As we examine the barriers to communication in part 1 of this book we will witness the further reduction of this quantity of information by the audience. We already have noted how many people ignore most items in the news and how even those items that are noticed are further reduced and reworked by each individual in the audience.

The final bits of information that each audience member carries about in his or her memory are an infinitely small proportion of the information out there in the real world. It is crucial for the professional journalist to understand this selection process and the variables that influence this progressive reduction of content at each step in the mass communication process. These variables affecting the flow of information—attitudes and interest, language patterns, perceptual habits, and interpersonal affiliations—define the barriers to effective communication.

These variables also spell out the two countervailing sets of influence on the communication process. The first set of influences resides in the audience and the community. They are the constraints on the mass communicator. All the barriers to effective communication posed by each individual in the mass communication audience are direct effects impinging on mass communication. And at a broader societal level, all the legal, economic, and cultural constraints influencing the mass communicator's performance are indirect manifestations of the audience's impact on mass communication. These audience-imposed constraints, both the direct and indirect ones, are the major focus of this book. Chapter 8 deals with them at the societal level.

But just as the audience affects mass communication messages, it is equally true that mass communication messages—the second set of influences—affect the audience. The world has been a very different place since the advent of mass communication with the penny press in the 1830s. Certainly, it has been a vastly different place since the introduction of radio in the 1920s and television in the 1940s. In fact, the real impetus for scholarly concern with mass communication and the amassing of empirical data on mass communication largely arose from a major concern over the effects of mass communication on its audience. Only recently has this imbalance been redressed by an increased concern over the constraints that the audience imposes on the mass media.

A balanced theory of mass communication, of course, must address both questions: What are the effects of mass communication on its audience? and What are the effects of the audience on mass communication? The emphasis here, however, is on the second question, the effects of the audience on mass communication, because this book is for journalists. If they are to succeed as mass communicators, they must be aware of the constraints that audiences can impose.

However, to present a full perspective on the mass communication process this book turns in chapter 9 from a detailed discussion of the barriers to effective mass communication—barriers imposed directly and indirectly by the audience—to a summary discussion of the effects and social impact of mass communication. This brief final chapter sketching the social impact of the mass media will, of necessity, only highlight this aspect of mass communication theory. A full explication of these effects, one paralleling the detail devoted here to audience constraints on the mass media, would require another volume.

To sum up, our first theme—the progressive reduction of information and content as we move through the mass communication process—provides an overview of the barriers to effective communication. It illustrates our central point that the production of messages does not equal communication. Our second theme—describing how the mass media and the audience have reciprocal effects on each other—places the discussion of communication barriers in context and illustrates the larger domain that a complete theory of mass communication must detail. In short, this book reviews the array of human behaviors that shape and determine the success or failure of our messages and previews the social impact of those messages in the marketplace.

PART ONE
THE AUDIENCE

2
Jabberwocky

'Twas brillig, and the slithy toves
  Did gyre and gimble in the wabe;
All mimsy were the borogoves,
  And the mome raths outgrabe.

LEWIS CARROLL

"Rose is a rose is a rose is a rose!" That famous line of poetry by Gertrude Stein does communicate to most American college students. They are accustomed to the style of modern poetry, and they certainly are familiar with what a rose is. But is a rose a rose to everyone? Clearly, the answer is No! For children in the South Pacific, for example, there is a major semantic problem here and with many other terms routinely employed in our writing.

Semantics is concerned with the link between the words used in messages and the objects or ideas these words represent. If the object or idea designated by a word is totally outside the experience of a reader or listener in the audience, then the message lacks meaning. It does not communicate. To children in the South Pacific and perhaps even to many children in deprived subcultures of this country, a rose is not a rose because the word doesn't designate anything within the child's experience.

For years the school children of those small, scattered South Pacific islands used textbooks and readers originally designed for American children. The messages in those beginning readers often were semantic nightmares, full of details about major metropolitan areas, their skyscrapers and subways, about freeways and hordes of automobiles, and about numerous other experiences totally alien to children in an island culture.

On a smaller scale, the same semantic problems exist for children in various regions and various ethnic and social subcultures of the United States who are routinely presented with words designating things totally beyond their experience. Now this is not to say that people are not enriched by exposure to new ideas and new experiences. Indeed they are! But the communicator must work at the introduction of new ideas. One cannot assume that understanding will result among children or adults from simple exposure to new words and terms. A rose is not always a rose!

LANGUAGE AS A BARRIER

Yet journalists use words daily that many audience members do not understand. For many persons in our audience we daily produce more of Lewis Carroll's jabberwocky. Language and words are the tools of the journalist, but they must be used with a high degree of precision if they are to do their job adequately. Put another way, language is a basic constraint on the communicator attempting to reach any audience, and it can be a formidable barrier to effective communication.

Good use of language is more than good spelling, careful syntax, and reasonable conformity to the semantics of the language, although those skills *do* contribute to audience understanding. Good use of language includes consideration of the language skills of the audience, as well as consideration of audience members' backgrounds and experience. It is concerned with what audience members will *understand* a message to mean, or whether they will understand at all. The audience members' level of comprehension thus imposes the major constraint on the journalist's use of words.

Reporters and editors need to consider this point because they can manipulate the language of their messages to compensate for audience capabilities. In fact, the ability of communicators to produce messages that overcome this fundamental barrier to communication is greater than their ability to cope with many of the other barriers in the communication process.

However, the daily press is full of examples indicating that little consideration has been given to the constraints of language. News organizations usually do a very thorough job of reporting on government, covering everything from the village board and state legislature to the Congress, White House, and numerous federal agencies in Washington. Everything from summaries of the local police court to the detailed decisions of the Supreme Court of the United States is reported.

This volume of detail, this attention to the numerous discrete acts and sessions of these government and judicial groups, requires reporters to under-

messages by counting only two elements, the average number of words in each sentence of the message and the average number of syllables per 100 words.* With these two pieces of information inhand, the writer can determine the level of difficulty, the readability, of his or her message with this simple arithmetic.

Reading ease = 206.835 − (.846 × average number of syllables per 100 words) − (1.015 × average sentence length)

In other words, multiply the average number of syllables per 100 words by .846 and subtract the resulting number from 206.835. From the number that remains, then subtract the average sentence length multiplied by 1.015. The number that results from this step is the reading ease score.

Never mind where all the numbers came from. That's a lesson in statistical analysis available in the references cited in the bibliography at the end of this book. What kind of results are obtained? Look at the news story leads in the two boxes. "An Armful of Art" is rather simply written. The crime rate story is much more complex. After scanning the messages, look at the Flesch formula calculated for each message and then look at table 2.2 for the interpretation of these scores. What is intuitively clear—that one message is much

* Rudolph Flesch, "A New Readability Yardstick," *Journal of Applied Psychology,* 32 (1948), 229. Copyright 1948 by the American Psychological Association. Reprinted by permission.

AN ARMFUL OF ART

Paul Richard

It is 11:14 sharp. Classes have just ended at John F. Kennedy High School in suburban Wheaton. Free period's just begun. The halls are full of Montgomery County teen-agers streaming from their classrooms, past the antique mural—the one that shows the Beatles and says "Make Love Not War"—toward the winter sunlight. There amidst the noise, the squeaking and bravado of adolescent voices, half a dozen high school kids display their tattoos.

Mike Melton has a snarling panther tattooed on his biceps. Mike Melton is 16. Kenny Hart and Bernie Fricke have eagles on their arms, and Bernie has two more tattoos. One of them says "Bernie," the other shows a tyke in boxing gloves and pompadour with the legend "Slugger." Greg Layton's arm says "Greg."

A wolf is howling at the moon, among dark clouds and pine trees, in Dave ("The Wolf Man") Wolfe's elaborate tattoo. . . .

Washington Post

Flesch Reading Ease Score = 54.44

SERIOUS CRIME DECREASES

Serious crime in the District of Columbia continued to decrease during November with substantial reductions due at least in part to a new program designed to remove repeat offenders from the streets, according to D.C. police officials.

Figures released this week show that the greatest yearly decrease—23 per cent—was in the number of armed robberies recorded during the first 11 months of 1976 compared to the same period last year. For the month of November this year, there was a 32 per cent reduction in armed robberies over November a year ago, the figures show. . . .

Washington Post

Flesch Reading Ease Score = 24.95

---

easier to understand than the other message—is stated with much greater precision when we use the formula and the scoring table.

Similar analyses and formulas have been developed to measure the listenability of broadcast news and other audio messages. Just as in the readability formulas, various elements—such as word and sentence length—are used to predict how well the average listener can understand or remember the broadcast message.

Words do make a difference. Language is a major constraint, but knowledgeable message producers can manipulate this constraint to their advantage through careful attention to the words and sentences they use.

In their attempts to map this aspect of the language barrier, communication theorists have counted words and quantified sentence characteristics in many ways. There are many different readability and listenability formulas

Table 2.2 Interpreting Reading Ease Scores*

Reading Ease Score	Description of Style	Typical Magazine	Average Syllables per 100 Words	Average Sentence Length in Words
0–30	Very difficult	Scientific	192 or more	29 or more
30–50	Difficult	Academic	167	25
50–60	Fairly difficult	Quality	155	21
60–70	Standard	Digests	147	17
70–80	Fairly easy	Slick fiction	139	14
80–90	Easy	Pulp fiction	131	11
90–100	Very easy	Comics	123 or less	8 or less

* Rudolf Flesch, "A New Readability Yardstick," *Journal of Applied Psychology*, 32 (1948), 230. Copyright 1948 by the American Psychological Association. Reprinted by permission.

available to the journalist. Focusing on two simple elements of writing, sylla-bles and numbers of words in a sentence, the Flesch formula is one easy way for a writer to calculate readability even during very rapid message construc-tion. But it was not clear until a great deal of research had been completed exactly which elements are good predictors of comprehension and understand-ing. For that matter, everyone still does not universally acclaim the Flesch formula as the best way to predict readability. But it is one of the highly useful maps of the language barrier.

A very different approach to readability and understanding, Cloze proce-dure, is more direct and intuitive in its approach, but does not lend itself to rapid calculation by the message producer. Extensive pretesting among the in-tended audience for the message is necessary.

Cloze procedure takes advantage of the *redundancy* in natural languages. One need not catch every word of a conversation or be able to make out every word in a printed message in order to understand the communication. Often the listener or reader can actually supply a missing or garbled word, because of the repetition and redundancy in our language. Context, both in terms of subject matter and in terms of syntactical form, supplies many cues about missing elements of language.

If I say to you, "It is raining cats and _____," the missing word *dogs* can be quickly supplied. Or if I say, "There goes the neighbor's _____ across the lawn," you can with *some* degree of success guess what the missing ele-ment is. Similarly, garbled or half-completed words can be guessed at rather successfully in real life as well as in crossword puzzles.

Cloze procedure uses this redundancy to study the readability of a mes-sage. In the usual procedure, words are randomly deleted from the message to be tested, and copy containing these blanks is presented to a representative sample of the audience for whom the message is intended. Sample members are simply asked to fill in as many of the missing blanks as possible.

The readability score for the message is the average percentage of blanks correctly filled in by the audience. If the message is written at an appropriate level for the intended audience, it will be able to supply a large proportion of the missing words. But if the message is too difficult, persons in the sample will not fill in or guess correctly very many of the blanks. Attention to redun-dancy, again from the viewpoint of the intended audience, is yet another way to cope with the language barrier in the communication process.

FEELING AND EMOTION

Understanding is one criterion for judging successful news communication. But people are not simple automatons who file away the facts conveyed in the daily news. Human response to words is far more than the logical processing of meanings. That is one part of verbal behavior, but the psychology of language also contains other major elements. Words, whether in news stories or in poetry, convey feelings and sentiments. They evoke emotion.

Journalists' descriptions of events and the major actors in those events both convey factual information about who, what, where, when, and why, and evoke impressions and opinions about those elements. The daily press is the major source of our attitudes and opinions about the actors and events on the world stage. Our affective responses of liking and disliking are created in large part from the elements of daily journalism.

Our professional standards in journalism, however, emphasize the *denotative* aspect of communication. The denotative meaning of a word is the object or idea referred to. It is the dictionary meaning of the word. But words also convey feelings. The words *person, man, leader,* and *crook* could all have the same denotative meaning in a news story. But these words convey vastly different impressions of the individual being described. Diplomats often haggle for hours over the *connotative* meanings of words. Or do they simply discuss those meanings? *Haggle* and *discuss* both denote a serious conversation of some duration, but have strikingly different connotative meanings.

The connotative aspect of a message often can be quite subtle. Take that frequently used word *said.* In the verbal behavior of the news writer, it has a high frequency of use. The word *said* itself is rather neutral; it really has no connotative meaning. But since the constant repetition of this word also becomes boring, journalists use a wide variety of synonyms to brighten up their writing. Among the literally dozens of synonyms, many have highly distinct connotative meanings.

At the writer's option, the word *said* can become *argued, insisted, maintained, charged, suggested,* or numerous other words with quite varied connotations. The choice of synonyms for *said*, or any other writer decision about which word to use in news copy, may be dictated by the writer's perception of the speaker's mood at the moment the statement was made. Or the choice may be nothing more than a random selection of different words to enhance the style of the news story. The choice also may be a deliberate manipulation of the connotative meaning of the news story!

Time magazine's choice of words to describe three presidents of the United States systematically painted very different pictures of those men. Never reticent at expressing its feelings and opinions of those in the news, *Time* subtly played on the connotative meanings of words to convey its interpretations and images of Harry S Truman, Dwight D. Eisenhower, and John F. Kennedy. The magazine's choice of adjectives, adverbs, and synonyms for the verb *said* conveyed consistent connotative messages during each administration.

Time's negative feelings about Truman were conveyed in such words and phrases as: *"said curtly," "barked Harry S Truman," "grinning slyly,"* and *"petulant, irascible President."* In contrast Eisenhower *"said with a happy grin," "chatted amiably," "said warmly,"* and *"paused to gather thought."*

Finally, there was the neutral handling of Kennedy, who in the pages of *Time* for the most part simply *said, announced,* and *concluded.*

The journalist's choice of words does more than convey simple understanding. Words also convey emotion and feeling. The ultimate message communicated to the audience is influenced by both the denotative and connotative meanings of the words used.

FROM WORDS TO EXPERIENCES

We now are ready to consider *conceptualization,* the audience's perspective of the world. This criterion for evaluating the effectiveness of communication is concerned with the total picture and larger meaning conveyed by all those words in our messages. Applying this criterion, the writer or member of the audience asks: What does it all mean? and What does it add up to? As we move to this broader criterion of successful communication, we become aware of additional barriers imposed by the language system.

Returning a moment to semantics—the relationship between a word and the object or idea it represents—we recall that there are great differences in the semantic skills of various writers and of various audience members. These individual differences affect the problem of understanding, of achieving a reasonable match between the semantic encoding skills of message producers and the semantic decoding skills of the audience.

A major problem arises when we try to match the signs and objects of one culture to the signs and objects of another culture. Different languages cut into reality in very different ways. They provide vastly different categories for encoding experiences in the real world, and they select very different aspects of situations for encoding in the language code. How language *per se* structures and organizes experience, how it becomes a determinant of our very own experiences, has intrigued philosophers and scientists for centuries.

Differences across languages in the manner of capturing and encoding reality are most striking. One study notes that the Hopi Indian language routinely distinguishes between pouring/spilling a *solid* versus a *liquid* while essentially ignoring whether the action was deliberate or accidental. English routinely makes the opposite distinction, ignoring the solid/liquid distinction while focusing on the nature of the action, whether it was deliberate *(pouring)* or accidental *(spilling).* There are numerous other examples from cross-cultural studies of language.

For the journalist preparing materials for international communication, the cross-cultural aspects of this constraint are crucial. Since message producers steeped in English prepare the majority of the news copy carried by the international wire services to nearly every nation of the world, this cultural constraint of language affects journalism worldwide.

used (for example, English and French in Canada), and in others significant minority language groups flourish (for example, several dialects of Spanish in the United States). Add to this the language differences among subcultures.

These constraints of language, determinants of understanding, emotional response, and conceptualization, are powerful editors of the communication process.

3
Seeing and Believing

Perception is a simple concept for the average person. The cliché "seeing is believing" points up the popular notion that one observes what is really, objectively there. Yet, occasional allegations of bias and distortion in journalists' news stories attest that individuals sometimes observe very different things in the same situation. Similarly, the unsuccessful or unexpected outcomes of numerous public information campaigns demonstrate that audience perceptions do not always match the expectations of message producers. The elements of raw sensory data, whether actual events or the words and pictures produced by journalists, are themselves insufficient to yield a coherent picture of the world as the normal person experiences it. What is perceived depends almost as much on the audience as it does on the message and the message producer.

This interaction of the perceiver and sensory input—whether direct sensory stimulation or the refined and edited input of mass communication—was described in chapter 2 at the cultural level. The Whorfian hypothesis, for example, details the influence of the perceiver's language on what is actually observed. Members of different cultures, or even subcultures, confronted with the same sensory experience do not perceive exactly the same thing because of the different ways in which languages categorize experience and organize reality.

What is true on a broad scale at the cultural level also is true at the individual level. Between individuals and their actual physical environment there is inserted what Walter Lippmann called the *pseudo-environment*. The world that the individual perceives and believes to be there, the pseudo-environment, is "a hybrid compounded of 'human nature' and 'conditions.'"

In the jargon of contemporary psychology, *human nature* is each individual's experiences over time, the picture of the world that has been created by his or her history of learning. *Conditions* are the objective stimuli to which an audience is exposed. In mass communication these stimuli, or collections of stimuli, are the messages that journalists produce and disseminate.

But out of these vast collections of stimuli only a small portion are actually perceived by the audience and become part of anyone's actual experience. The world outside and the pictures in our heads are vastly different environments. The small portion of the external world actually perceived is not a random sample of what is available. Which stimuli are selected by an individual depends on three major factors: (1) the nature of the stimuli, (2) previous audience experience and learning, and (3) the structure and process of human perception. The interaction of these factors results in each individual's view of the world and accounts for each individual's response to news messages. A news audience is not a passive *tabula rasa* waiting to be inscribed with the daily news. Audiences are psychologically active individuals who organize their own idiosyncratic pictures of the world. News messages are only the raw material for this process.

SELECTING FROM REALITY

If one did attend to each bit of sensory input, the world would be a "buzzing, blooming confusion." Only by selecting samples from this barrage of information impinging on the senses—and imposing some organization on this sample—can each person efficiently cope with the environment. Since a vast array of stimuli are available to an individual for the construction of meaningful patterns, but only a few stimuli are actually used by each member of the audience, the journalist needs some knowledge of the selection process that takes place. Which stimuli are most likely to be sampled?

News stories are filled with details. The names and descriptions of many persons, institutions, and events are the facts from which the daily news is constructed. Some politicians, celebrities, government groups, and events are highly familiar to news audiences due to their constant appearance in the news. Others each day are unfamiliar and new. Especially for newly emerging issues, names, and events in the news, it is critical to know how the journalist's descriptions will be perceived by the audience. Out of the numerous attributes of these persons, issues, and events that are elaborated in the news, which ones actually will be selected by the audience?

Fortunately, in the case of attributes of elements in the news, there are some very regular patterns in this selection process. The nature of the stimulus, or to be specific, the nature of the attribute, makes a great difference in how effectively it can be communicated to a general audience. Such attributes or characteristics as *time, physical dimensions,* and *quantity* occur frequently in news stories, yet none of these are very readily recalled by readers of those stories. On the other hand, less frequently cited attributes such as *sensation, color,* and other *physical properties* are easily recalled by readers.

Habit leads people, both audiences and message producers, to select some attributes much more frequently than others for encoding in their messages. That is one psychological constraint. But in the subsequent recall of those message elements, of those attributes, there is a kind of novelty effect so that the less frequently cited attributes are better remembered. The *nature of the stimuli* does make a difference in what is perceived and remembered.

PREVIOUS LEARNING
AND EXPERIENCE

We use the term *effecting closure* to mean completing or filling in what is incomplete or unclear. Just as audiences effect closure upon gaps and ambiguities in the actual words and language of a message, they also effect closure upon ambiguities in information and details of messages presented to them.

This natural human tendency is one basis for rumor. The information transmitted in the rumor satisfies a psychological need for closure or completeness. Rumor and hard news of the journalistic variety are psychological cousins since they both dispel ambiguity and satisfy a need for orientation to the surrounding environment.

Because of space and time limitations and because of its emphasis on the new, a typical daily news report on a particular topic is not a complete description and discussion of that topic. As the reader or viewer assimilates this partial account, he or she feels a natural psychological tendency to complete the account, to supply enough of the missing details to yield a sense of completeness. In this process of closure, individuals apply their own unique experience to the task. People supply these missing elements in line with their own backgrounds.

Stereotyping affords another example of this process of closure at work. A stereotype is a collection of attributes describing a person, group, or institution. There is great regularity in the catalog of descriptive attributes routinely applied to Frenchmen, Germans, Chinese, college professors, used car dealers, and bankers. So when someone is identified with one of these categories, an entire set of attributes is more or less automatically attributed to that individual whether the individual actually possesses those characteristics or not. This is another instance of effecting closure, of supplying additional information to that conveyed by the messages in order to achieve a "complete" picture.

The existence of stereotyping behavior among news audiences further illustrates the discrepancy between the world outside and the pictures in people's heads. The basic criticism of stereotyping, of course, is this lack of correspondence. Not all college professors are absent-minded. Not all used car dealers are untrustworthy.

A classic perception experiment by Allport and Postman helps further illustrate this point. The subjects in the experiment were shown a series of photographs in which typical stereotypic situations were reversed or in which the information shown in the picture was incomplete. One of these pictures, for example, included a white man with a straight razor accosting a black man, portions of signs with common street names, and advertisements in which familiar names such as Lucky Strikes had been changed to Lucky Strakes.

As predicted, subjects who viewed this picture and others like it tended to describe its content in terms of familiar or anticipated experiences. The incomplete street signs were filled out, familiar brand names were recalled, and the razor typically was perceived in the hands of the black. Learned stereotypes and expectations overrode the actual content of the picture. Stereotyping and the human tendency toward closure both illustrate the effects of *previous learning and experience* on what is perceived.

SELECTIVE PERCEPTION

A key part of each individual's experience that influences his or her perceptions is the set of previously acquired *attitudes* and *opinions*. Stereotypes straddle the boundary between *cognitions,* our mental pictures of the world about us, and affective *attitudes,* our feelings and evaluations of persons, issues, and situations in the world around us.

As we have said, every element of a message is not equally attended to. Among other factors, each individual's attitudes enter into this selection process. Favorably regarded items in the news are more likely to be noted and recalled than unfavorably regarded ones. Or to put it another way, the perception and interpretation of something in the news, especially if it is ambiguous or incomplete in any way, are most likely to be made congruent with the viewer's or reader's attitude. For example, audience perceptions and interpretations of the numerous Watergate news stories and of President Nixon's statements at that time were quite different for Democrats and Republicans and for supporters and opponents of Nixon.

Selective perception frequently has been cited as a major factor in the failure, or limited success, of public information campaigns. Preexisting attitudes brought to the communication situation by the audience, especially strongly held attitudes, can mitigate, alter, or even reverse the intended meaning of a message.

All three outcomes are present, for example, in a famous experiment by Eunice Cooper and Marie Jahoda in which highly prejudiced subjects were exposed in the laboratory to cartoons ridiculing prejudice and stereotypes.

Rather than accept the antiprejudice messages, subjects tended to do the following: they avoided any understanding of what the message really was, they invalidated the message by claiming factual errors or personal exceptions, and, they totally changed the frame of reference so as to make the message acceptable. Audience attitudes can pose a formidable barrier to effective communication.

Psychologist Leon Festinger reports a similar outcome from a study of audience evaluations of the surgeon general's warning on the hazards of cigarette smoking. The more favorable each individual's attitude was toward smoking, as indexed by the number of cigarettes smoked each day, the less convinced he or she was that an actual link had been established between smoking and lung cancer.

A classic study of a roughly contested Dartmouth-Princeton football game also illustrates this idea of selective perception with the kind of event that journalists observe and describe to others. In that contest Princeton's star player left the game with a broken nose in the second quarter. A Dartmouth player left with a broken leg in the third quarter. Not counting a number of plays in which both teams were penalized, the statistics showed that Princeton, the winner, was penalized twenty-five yards. and Dartmouth seventy yards. The differing perceptions of what really happened that November afternoon were documented by a study in which groups of Dartmouth and Princeton undergraduates viewed a film of the game and checked off the number of rule infractions they observed. Several comparisons can be made from the findings reported in table 3.1.

Both groups of students essentially agreed on the number of infractions committed by the Princeton team. But this is their only point of agreement. The Princeton students attributed more than twice as many infractions to the Dartmouth team as did the Dartmouth students. Similarly, while the Dartmouth students observed about an equal number of infractions by each team, the Princeton students saw Dartmouth committing twice as many infractions as the Princeton team.

The cliché goes: "Seeing is believing." Sometimes, the behavioral sequence becomes: "Believing is seeing."

Selective perception, which we have been discussing here, is concerned with the actual details of the message, with how it is perceived by the individual. Another, prior barrier, *selective exposure,* to be detailed in chapter 4, deals with an individual's selection of a message or set of messages from the range of those available. A person may or may not choose to watch the local news on channel 6. A person may or may not be in the habit of reading certain magazines. Patterns of selective exposure are instances of systematic nonexposure, perhaps active avoidance, of certain messages or sets of messages.

But even if this barrier of selective exposure is overcome by the communicator, exposure to a message in no way guarantees perception of all its elements. Even though a person views a certain news story on television or

Table 3.1 They Saw a Game

	Average Number of Infractions Observed Against	
	Dartmouth Team	Princeton Team
Dartmouth Students	4.3	4.4
Princeton Students	9.8	4.2

* Adapted from Albert Hastorf and Hadley Cantril, "They Saw a Game: A Case Study," *Journal of Abnormal and Social Psychology*, 49 (1954), 131. Copyright 1954 by the American Psychological Association. Reprinted by permission.

scans it in the evening newspaper, he or she is unlikely to actually perceive all the details. And even when exposure to particular parts of the message is guaranteed, there still are individual differences in what is perceived. The perceptions reported in the Cooper-Jahoda experiment with cartoons, the viewing of the Princeton-Dartmouth football game, and the study of the surgeon general's warning on cigarette smoking all underscore the differences in perceptions among members of the audience. To the extent that there is a pattern in the perception of these message elements, particularly to the extent that the pattern is determined by previous experiences or present attitudes, there is selective perception.

SELECTIVE RETENTION

There is at least one more phase of selectivity—*memory and retention*. Even though a person is exposed to a message and actually perceives its elements—this is frequently the case for advertisements in saturation campaigns—over time there still can be selectivity in what is remembered. Here again, attitudes and opinions play a key role in what is actually retained. Social psychology experiments demonstrate that the individual's repertoire of experiences and attitudes actively shapes what is remembered from messages over time.

In one experiment, groups of pro-Communist and anti-Communist college students were exposed weekly for a period of five weeks to both a pro–Soviet Union and anti–Soviet Union message. Their progress in learning the anti-Soviet passage is charted in figure 3.1. Clearly, the anti-Communist group, for whom the message was compatible, learned its content more rapidly. In the second stage of the experiment, stretching over another five weeks, the two groups of students were tested weekly for their recall of the passage. Here again, the group for whom the message was compatible retained more of the message over time. Although not charted here, similar results were obtained for the pro-Soviet message. As expected from the previous discussion of selective

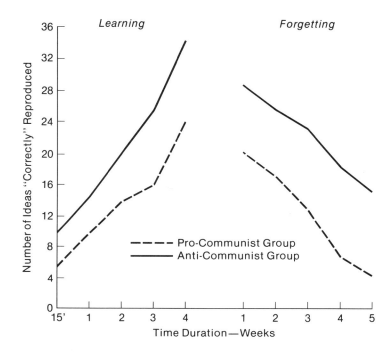

Fig. 3.1 Learning and Forgetting of Anti-Communist Message (Adapted from J. M. Levine and Gardner Murphy, "The Learning and Forgetting of Controversial Material," *Journal of Abnormal and Social Psychology,* 38 [1943], 513.)

perception, the compatible message was better learned, and in line with the idea of selective retention, the compatible message also was better retained.

Numerous attitudes and opinions result from each individual's previous history of learning and experience. These attitudes and opinions can affect both what is initially perceived—*selective perception*—and what is remembered over time—*selective retention.*

Two basic perceptual constraints on effective communication now have been enumerated. First, there is the differential impact of different message stimuli. The various descriptive attributes of persons, events, and issues are selectively encoded and recalled from messages on the basis of their strength as *stimuli.* But second, we also noted how *each individual's behavioral repertoire* exerts tremendous selectivity on what is actually communicated. Stereotyping, tendency toward closure, selective perception, and selective recall each illustrate the effects of an individual's previous learning and experience on perception, effects that pose barriers to our attempts to communicate messages to an audience.

There is yet a third source of constraint: the human perceptual structure and process through which message stimuli are sensed and on which the behavioral repertoire exerts its influence. In short, we must examine the apparatus of perception and how it operates psychologically.

Perception psychologist Donald Broadbent postulates a two-part perceptual apparatus that takes into account and explains the evidence of selective perception: an early, preliminary state in the nervous system where sensory information can pass *simultaneously,* and a later stage that can only pass bits of information *successively*. This distinction is based on extensive scientific evidence that bits of information reaching the senses simultaneously nevertheless will subsequently be processed successively.

For example, Broadbent modified the usual memory-span experiment— how much a person can recall—so that subjects wore earphones connected to two separate channels. Two lists of digits were presented simultaneously. Subjects were asked to reproduce in any order they chose all six digits that had been presented. In most cases subjects reproduced all six digits, but presented all the information from one channel before presenting any information received through the other channel.

If the digit series were 723 and 945, the response always was either 723945 or 945723. It was never 792435 or any other integrated response. When asked to alternate channels and give the digits in the actual order they were received, subjects experienced great difficulty and were unable to comply in most cases. Similar results were obtained when information was presented simultaneously via the eye and ear.

In another experiment on the order in which things are recalled, subjects viewed pairs of cards through a tachistoscope, a type of slide machine that exposes a picture to the person in the experiment for only a fraction of a second. In this experiment each card shown on the tachistoscope contained several objects of the same shape and color. The six facts to be reported by each subject were the number of objects on each card, the shape on each card, and the color used on each card.

If subjects were instructed to concentrate on one of the three dimensions in describing what they had seen on the cards, errors tended to be made on the other two dimensions. Even when only the order of recall for the three attributes was given in the instructions, similar results were obtained—errors were made on the last dimensions reported. Since these instructions for order of recall were presented *subsequent* to viewing, no selective factor was operative at the actual time of viewing. The selectivity that appeared empirically in the responses is due to memory and the cognitive processing of the information that has taken place.

In other words, the results of this experiment are evidence that the selective nature of perception does not appear at the moment of stimulation, the first stage of the perceptual process, but only in the subsequent processing of this

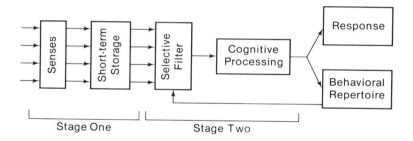

Fig. 3.2 A Model of the Perception Process (Adapted from Donald E. Broadbent, *Perception and Communication* [London: Pergamon Press, 1958], p. 299. Reprinted with permission from Pergamon Press.)

information at stage two (fig. 3.2). In the initial stage where information can pass simultaneously, everything registered on the senses goes into preliminary storage. Then the information moves from this preliminary storage into the second, processing stage where information is handled sequentially or successively. It is in this sequential ordering of the information that selective perception takes place. Here such psychological factors as attitudes and previous audience experience and learning exert an editing influence on which things are admitted for actual cognitive processing by the individual.

"Seeing is believing" *may* be a correct description for the behavior of many people in our audiences. Often people do perceive what is really there. But this observation is not very comforting to the communicator who is aware of all the factors that *can* influence what each individual perceives in our news stories and other messages. Clearly, what each individual perceives is often somewhat different—sometimes, extremely different—from what the journalist intends to communicate. Perception is a major barrier to effective mass communication.

4
The Active Audience

Two years after the founding of the United Nations, a campaign was launched to better inform the people of Cincinnati about the world organization. The intent was to demonstrate "how a community may become so intelligently informed on world affairs as to be a dynamic force in the creation of an ordered and eventually a peaceful world."

To accomplish this end the campaign sponsors designed numerous messages about the UN and developed elaborate means to distribute these messages. Local newspapers played up news and features about the UN during the six-month campaign. Radio stations broadcasted facts about the world organization, one of them using 150 spot-programs a week. Supplementary literature was distributed through Parent Teacher Associations, schools, churches, women's clubs, and other similar groups. In all, approximately 60,000 pieces of literature were distributed. A speakers bureau was set up, and hundreds of documentary films were shown. The slogan, "Peace Begins with the United Nations—the United Nations Begins with You," was exhibited on matchbooks, blotters, street car cards and other public displays. The message, it seemed, was everywhere in Cincinnati.

The project sponsors, however, later concluded they hadn't done much communicating. It wasn't that the message was faulty, they decided, or that the distribution system itself was flawed. Rather, they concluded, many of the people of Cincinnati simply weren't participating in the communication process.

In fact, studies of the Cincinnati project showed, very little new information about the UN reached the audience. At the beginning of the campaign, social scientists from the National Opinion Research Center (NORC) found that 30 percent of the residents knew nothing about the main purpose of the United Nations. After the campaign—despite the slogans, the media spots, and the vast amount of literature distributed—a similar proportion still was unable to give a reasonable answer. The number of people, for example, who knew of the UN veto and could explain how it worked remained constant during the campaign. The inescapable conclusion, the social scientists told the campaign sponsors, was that the level of information in Cincinnati about the UN did not change very much during the period of the campaign.

The researchers, however, offered some explanations for this lack of change. They had discovered certain barriers to communications—though they didn't use those words—that the audience members, perhaps inadvertently, had erected. The scientists had instructed the project sponsors early in the information campaign to attempt to reach the poor, the relatively uneducated, and the elderly in Cincinnati. Those groups were the least informed about the UN. But the postcampaign study indicated that those audience members most in need of the information, at least from the point of view of the sponsors, were least likely to remember having been exposed to the message. The poor, the elderly, and the uneducated were not interested in international events or the UN. Uninterested people generally paid less attention to the campaign than did the interested.

Attitudes of audience members toward the world organization also were related to the amount of attention they paid to the campaign. Those most exposed were, in general, the most favorably disposed. The evidence was that the precampaign attitudes were the really important ones. People most favorable to the UN *before* the campaign even started were more likely to pay attention to the messages about it. *Selective exposure* was a barrier to effective communication.

The Cincinnati study, and others like it, had dramatic impact on the thinking in the fields of mass communication and journalism. Before that time, many researchers and practicing journalists had thought the media had almost unlimited potential for influencing audience members. Many viewed the media as a hypodermic syringe, capable of injecting into its passive audience any message the syringe contained. There might be an outcry on occasion, but such feedback changed the impact of the media only if the message was changed. Message construction and distribution, in this view, were the key determinants of communication.

This old view, of course, gave considerable support to the journalist who was concerned only with style and message content. He or she liked the notion that if the message was well formulated, and someone made sure it was transmitted, communication had taken place. But social scientists argued that the

Cincinnati experience indicated otherwise. Audience members have considerable control over communication. In recognition of this power, social scientist Raymond Bauer labeled the receivers of mass communication the "obstinate audience." The role of the audience in communication needed to be considered in detail, Bauer said.

Bauer's choice of a descriptive term for the audience may be a bit unfortunate. It seems to suggest that the balance of power is with the receivers of media messages. What was intended, however, was something else. Communication results from an interaction in which two parties expect to give and take, Bauer said. Professional communicators who ignore the characteristics and orientations of the audience members do so at the peril of actual communication, or information transmittal.

In other words, Bauer's perspective is that mass communication, if it is to be successful, must take on many characteristics of interpersonal communication. Audience members must be able to give feedback. Media practitioners must be sensitive to the information contained in the feedback. The give and take can result in understanding, or real communication.

Novelist Kurt Vonnegut, Jr., expressed a similar notion in *Cat's Cradle,* a surrealistic account of the end of the world. Humanity is organized by an external force into teams called *Karasses,* says John, the narrator of the story. Teammates work together toward some goal, though members may never know of the bond that holds them. Some people, however, think they are members of a *karass,* though they are not, and try to behave accordingly. A false *karass* is called a *granfalloon,* which gives some indication of its characteristics.

In a sense, professional communicators who ignore their audience members run the risk of creating a communicative *granfalloon.* The journalists may think there is a communicative bond, and behave accordingly. But the other people in the perceived network are not tuned into the message. Without them, the communication fails.

Social scientists have accumulated considerable evidence of how audience members approach communication, and the conscientious communicator can turn to that evidence. The evidence forms part of the behavioral stylebook we've talked about and can help journalists avoid some of the pitfalls of communicative *granfalloons.*

SELECTIVE EXPOSURE

In the early 1950s, psychologists Leon Festinger, Henry Riecken, and Stanley Schachter read a news story telling of a woman who claimed to have received a prophecy about a major impending flood. The deluge, according to the woman, would submerge the West Coast and create an inland sea stretching from the Arctic Circle to the Gulf of Mexico. The flood would destroy much of the continent, including the area where the woman lived.

These psychologists previously had noticed some interesting consistencies in the behaviors of members of millennial or messianic movements. They decided to join a group of the flood prophesier's followers to better understand the phenomenon. The psychologists were particularly interested in what happened in the group when the prophecy failed.

Mrs. Keech, the fictionalized name of the woman who claimed to have received the message from outer space, had been given specific instructions on how she and her followers might avoid the disaster. They were to prepare themselves for a visitor who would escort them to a flying saucer that would carry them from the flood to a place of safety, probably in outer space. The escort would arrive on the eve of the flood and pick up the believers, assembled in a group to await the fulfillment of the prophecy.

As the psychologists expected, the designated arrival time passed without contact by the visitor from outer space. At first, there was no visible reaction from the group members. But gradually, the atmosphere changed to despair and confusion. The assembled group members began to reexamine the earlier communications to determine if any mistakes had been made. At one point, the group seemed near dissolution. The escort had not arrived, and no explanation had been found.

But soon Mrs. Keech summoned everyone to attention and announced that she had just received another message: because of the faith of the group, the floods would not occur, and no escort was needed. The explanation was received with enthusiasm. The prophecy had not failed, despite the evidence, because an *explanation* of that evidence had been offered. In fact, group members began to proselytize about their beliefs publicly, arguing that the apparent disconfirmation of their beliefs was in fact a confirmation.

The ability of the group members to distort the evidence at hand was fascinating to the psychologists. It fit the pattern of events they had discovered from historical examination of such groups. And it sparked ideas about human ability to deal with the external world. The observations formed the basis for a theory about how individuals reduce cognitive dissonance, or psychological discomfort, by selectively perceiving the world around them, selectively exposing themselves to that world, and selectively retaining aspects of the information received. Since selective perception and retention were discussed in detail in chapter 3, selective exposure is our major concern here.

While the theory of cognitive dissonance has become more elaborate as the result of continuing research, its basic tenets can be illustrated relatively simply. Let's assume you voted for a certain candidate for high office, and maybe even contributed time and money to his campaign. Perhaps you really liked him and thought he'd make a swell official. You thought him honest, trustworthy, beyond rebuke. Then, four or five months after the election, evidence started to mount that your man wasn't all of those things. In fact, he was none of them. The guy turned out to be a crook.

Short of changing your evaluation of the candidate—the one you invested in so heavily during the campaign—you could handle evidence like this in several ways. You could distort the evidence: maybe the guy's friends were crooks, but certainly he wasn't. That is *selective perception,* and it may just work. Otherwise, you could avoid reading about the new revelations, avoid listening to the broadcasts, maybe forbid your friends from talking with you about him. That would be *selective exposure,* and it might work as well. Finally, as the theory notes, you could conveniently forget parts of what you did learn. That's *selective retention,* and it sometimes seems to work.

For supporters and former supporters of Richard Nixon, that scenario may ring true. In the months following the 1972 campaign, several studies show, many people did all of the things listed above. And people who voted for Nixon in that campaign were more likely to do them than people who had not. For some, the defenses seemed to work. For others they didn't. Many eventually said they made a mistake when they voted. Others simply changed their recollections of how they actually had voted in 1972. Studies of the Watergate era show that if Senator George McGovern had received all the votes people said they gave him, the 1972 landslide wouldn't have been.

Reactions to Watergate were, of course, very complex, and the illustration above is only that—an illustration. But awareness of the potential selectivity on the part of audience members is crucial. And it helps to examine in some detail just what is known about the pervasiveness of that kind of activity. Selectivity can be a major barrier to communication.

The idea of *selective exposure* didn't originate with Festinger's work. The NORC researchers studying the Cincinnati information campaign on the United Nations thought selective exposure a reasonable explanation for the project's lack of effect. Important political studies by researchers in the 1940s also suggested that people exposed themselves to messages about political campaigns in different ways depending on their preferences for those contents. And selective exposure has been offered as a general explanation for why it is easier to demonstrate effects of persuasive messages in laboratory experiments than in studies conducted in real-world settings. Laboratory settings usually preclude selective exposure. Real life settings do not.

Social scientists agree that people who hold attitudes compatible with those presented in a given message often will be more likely to expose themselves to that message than audience members with differing attitudes. This correlation between attitude and exposure has been demonstrated in a multitude of settings. Nearly twice as many Republicans as Democrats were found to have viewed a Republican candidate's telethon during the 1958 California gubernatorial race, for example. The classic studies of voters and mass communication in Erie County, Ohio, and Elmira, New York, also demonstrated the relationship. In the 1940 Erie County study, about two-thirds of the respondents who did not change their voting intention during the campaign were exposed predominantly to materials favoring their side.

Newspaper readers in several locations have been found to prefer the paper that takes editorial stands most comparable to their own. And as indicated, several studies of viewer attention to the Watergate story have shown this kind of selectivity. Even the Senate Erwin committee hearings, table 4.1 shows, were less likely to be of interest to Republicans than Democrats or Independents.

There is considerable debate among social scientists, however, about the cause of this *de facto* selectivity. In several of the studies mentioned, it is possible to demonstrate that selectivity may have resulted not from a *desire* to seek supportive information, but from other forces. In the Erie County study, for example, the media carried considerably more Republican-oriented material than Democratically focused stories. And since Republicans were dominant in the county, the observed selectivity may have resulted simply from the imbalance in the information available.

In the United Nations study, as well, the observed selectivity may have resulted from the relationship between education and attitude held. Those persons who were better educated were more favorably inclined toward the UN and more likely to expose themselves to the materials of the campaign. Consequently, it is difficult to know whether the educational level of the Cincinnati residents, their attitudes, or both their educational level and their attitudes led them to the United Nations materials.

These ambiguities, coupled with mixed results from later experimental studies based on Festinger's theory, have led some researchers to challenge the notion that people *purposely* expose themselves only to information supportive to their beliefs and attitudes. From the practicing journalist's perspective, however, the debate over the cause of the oft-observed selectivity is not as important as the existence of this selectivity. The professional communicator must keep in mind that any given story is not likely to be read by all persons in the audience. Those most favorably inclined to the content of the story are, in general, more likely to be the readers.

The selectivity processes are important barriers to effective communication. Selective exposure, discussed in some detail here, as well as the selectivity of perception and retention previously discussed in chapter 3, may result in a lack of understanding on the part of many audience members.

Table 4.1 Interest in Senate Watergate Hearings (Summer 1973)*

	Percent with "Great Deal" of Interest in Ongoing Hearings	Percent with Less Interest
Republicans (n = 360)	26	74
Independents (n = 490)	37	63
Democrats (n = 650)	35	65

* Adapted from *The Gallup Opinion Index*, 97 (July 1973), 7. Reprinted by permission.

THE CHRONIC "KNOW-NOTHINGS"

After several studies of information campaigns, social scientists Herbert Hyman and Paul Sheatsley began to notice something rather disturbing: the people who knew little about the particular topic of an information campaign after it was carried out also were likely to know little about other kinds of public events. In other words, there seemed to be a group of people who just didn't get the message—any message—regardless of what the planners of the information campaign tried. This group formed a core of chronic *know nothings*.

The notion isn't really very complex, and almost every practicing journalist has noticed it. The courthouse reporter who spends hours pouring over court records, talking with sources, and sitting through a court hearing to prepare a news story in an important local case, only to realize the next morning quite a few of his or her nonprofessional friends didn't know a thing about it, has experienced this phenomenon. The reporter probably didn't call the friends by the name chosen by Hyman and Sheatsley. But seasoned reporters get used to the idea that much of what they write will be unknown to a large number of people. And many of these will be the same people day after day.

Many of those who don't read the stories or see the news broadcasts are those most in need of the information. The least informed members of the population are usually the ones who don't do what they need to do to become informed—and of course that is why they are uninformed in the first place. It is a cycle with some serious consequences for our society and the democratic process.

Several studies have shown that as news coverage of an issue increases during a given period, the better educated members of the population tend to acquire this information at a faster rate than members with lower levels of education. As a result of this differential acquisition of information, the *gaps in knowledge* between groups in the population increase rather than decrease. In other words, the informationally rich get richer while the informationally poor remain the same. The discrepancy results from the fact that the better educated are the ones most likely to expose themselves to the incoming information.

This gap in knowledge seems less likely to occur, however, when the information being transmitted is about a highly controversial topic. In other words, when everybody is affected by the information, almost everyone pays attention to it. The gap is likely to be largest when people think the information has little impact on their lives.

For the working journalist, this tendency has several implications. To attempt to overcome the problem, messages should be designed to show the relevance of the information to the daily lives of the audience members. Foreign affairs news, for example, unless it is tied directly to local problems, will be read only by the better educated. And since the information in these stories may ultimately be of great consequence to all audience members, efforts should be made to counteract the tendency of those who know little to make few attempts to learn more. Several studies have now shown that when information campaigns are designed with this in mind, it is possible to reach the informationally poor.

UTILITY
OF THE INFORMATION

Most practicing journalists have some rough ideas before the paper actually hits the streets about which subgroups in the audience are most likely to read the various stories. And often, these hunches are right. Lawyers and other members of the courthouse crowd would be expected to read more stories written about legal activities than would members of the audience at large. People who go out on the town regularly would be expected to read more entertainment pieces. Older people would be expected to read the obituaries more often. People seem to expose themselves to those parts of mass communication they think will be most useful to them.

In general, communication research has borne out this expectation. Students have been found to be more interested in reading about the merits and demerits of a particular examination they had decided to take than about an examination they had rejected. Experimental subjects informed they would have to either offer reasons in support of a decision they had made on a given topic or rebut opposing arguments have been found to seek information most useful for the task assigned them, regardless of the position they had originally taken on the issue. The *perceived utility* of the information overrode any inclinations toward selectivity they might originally have had.

In each of these examples, perceived utility results from some specific task awaiting those involved in the study. The students knew of the upcoming exam. And subjects in the other example were told they would have a task to perform after they were given the opportunity to read some of the available materials.

Everyday life presents a host of comparable situations. We see the signs of summer, so we begin to pay more attention to stories in the local papers about recreational facilities and programs. We need new clothes, so we are more inclined to read the advertisements for local clothing outlets. Recognizing the need to drive a certain route to work in the morning, we pay attention to the morning traffic condition broadcast. The tasks in our lives help determine to which information we will pay attention.

A group of less specific tasks we face each day, as well, also seems to affect the perceived utility of information. Often, we feel the need for certain kinds of information because we anticipate some situation involving other people where that information might be useful. We might intend to use the information to demonstrate our competence and thereby improve our social standing. Or the information might be necessary just to continue in a social gathering. Certainly a person belonging to a discussion group focusing on community problems will lose standing if he or she does not keep informed on developments in the community.

Information also can be used to flatter or embarrass. If you want to impress someone, you try to keep informed on topics they like to talk about so you can enter into the conversation meaningfully. And some information has value because it puts people on the spot. Because we anticipate social interaction and interpersonal communication, we appreciate the usefulness of certain kinds of information and the uselessness of others.

SALIENCE OF A TOPIC

People often are interested in certain news stories, not so much because the information will be useful in the future, but because of exposure to similar topics in the past. Because of the exposure, the topic has become conspicuous, or salient to them. In other words, a kind of habit has formed, and old habits are hard to break. Expressions such as "He's really interested in politics" or "Baseball is his life" are summary comments on interest. Interest in a topic is related to exposure to information on that topic.

People who learn about a news event on the radio or from friends often have been found to turn later to other sources, such as newspapers, to learn more.

An unpublished study conducted in Syracuse, New York, after the 1976 vice presidential debate illustrates this rather clearly. The data, shown in table 4.2, indicate that those persons who viewed the first-ever televised debate between vice presidential candidates were more likely than nonviewers to read later about the encounter in newspapers. The same thing seems to have happened after the 1976 presidential debates as well.

In general, people who use newspapers heavily for public affairs information are also likely to use the other media, such as magazines and television, for the same kind of information. And numerous studies have shown that those people who are most interested in politics are the ones who report having paid most attention to the political stories appearing in the media.

The process seems to be cyclical. The media present various stories on a topic. An individual reader, perhaps because he or she knows friends will be talking about the stories, starts reading. The initial stories stimulate new interest in the topic, and additional reading takes place.

The journalist must keep in mind that the most interested people, those who have read similar stories in the past, are the most likely readers of stories

Table 4.2 Reading about the 1976 Vice Presidential Debate

	Percent Reading "Most" or "Some" Newspaper Stories about Debate	Percent Reading "Almost None" of the Newspaper Stories about Debate
Watched Vice Presidential Debate (n = 124)	51	49
Did Not Watch Debate (n = 74)	42	58

he or she is writing. But efforts should be made to increase the size of this group to further the goal of successful communication.

PERSONALITY FACTORS

Psychologists often talk about personality variables and how they affect the way individuals behave. While the term personality is used in many different ways, one common view is to think of personality as a trait or orientation that leads people to behave in consistent ways across *time* and *setting*. In other words, a personality trait is a summary description of the way a person approaches life.

Some research has been done on how such traits affect an individual's use of the mass media. A person's mental capability, usually referred to as Intelligence Quotient (IQ), is related to use of the media. As would be expected, those with lower IQs use the print media less. We also would expect those with low IQs to use different parts of the media than those with higher IQ scores, but there is little direct evidence to bear this out where *adults* are concerned. Studies of *children* have shown those with lower IQs continue with heavy entertainment viewing of television, which usually begins at an early age, as they get older while the more intelligent children begin to shift to reality-oriented fare.

An early study of listeners to daytime radio series found no personality differences between those who listened and those who did not. Though this study did not focus on news content of the media, there is little reason to expect the findings to differ where newspaper entertainment-type features are concerned.

Studies of college students have found only mild relationships between several personality factors and exposure to public affairs content of the media. Students high in dogmatism do seem to be slightly more likely to use public affairs materials than students low on that personality measure.

These limited findings suggest personality may not be the real, or functional, explanation for the media behaviors under question. Rather, situational factors, such as topic salience or perceived utility of information, may override the influence of personality.

USES AND GRATIFICATIONS

An alternative approach to examining personality factors, and one more firmly based in the research literature, is to focus on the *reasons* audience members have for using the media, or specific aspects of the media. This research tradition, which shares our concern here with audience orientations toward mass communicated messages, developed historically as a reaction to the hypodermic model of mass media effects. Rather than focusing on what the media do to their audience members, researchers in this theoretical tradition ask what *uses* audience members make of the messages and what *gratifications* audience members seek.

Many theorists refer to this as a functionalist approach to the study of the communication process. The central question of communication, these theorists argue, is: *What function do the media play for audience members?* Questions aimed at uncovering effects of messages from the communicator's point of view are backwards, these theoriests argue, because such questions ignore the active role of audience members in the communication process. Although they often seem to underplay the role of the communicator and thereby run the risk of seeing all mass communications from too limited a perspective, these theorists have provided some important insights into the part audience members play in the communication process. They have helped identify yet other barriers to communication.

Some years ago a strike by the delivery men of New York's major newspapers effectively deprived that city's residents of their daily newspapers for over two weeks. Most readers were forced to find other sources of information—or do without. For researchers interested in the reasons behind the usual habits of newspaper readership, the strike was a near ideal opportunity to find out about reader uses of the newspaper medium and the gratifications sought.

Most regular readers reported they missed their papers intensely. When asked what parts of the paper were missed most, readers overwhelmingly said the news. Of particular interest were news stories on the national and local level and international developments relating to the war. Readers also said they missed the advertisements. Those interviewed said they had been forced to listen more intensely to news broadcasts to learn about the world around them.

The researchers also learned that newspaper readers place fairly high value on their reading habits. In other words, they think reading is the *right* thing to do. They also know it is the *socially acceptable* thing to do. But probes of the responses convinced the researchers a core of readers finds the newspaper *indispensable* as a means of learning about world affairs. For others, however, the motivation to read was less "noble." Many were seeking escape from their own problems, simple relaxation, and entertainment. Others were seeking social prestige; aware of the value of public affairs in conversation, they followed their newspapers closely. Some were simply seeking help with everyday problems. Newspapers provide details on fashion, recipes, weather forecasts, and other information wanted by many respondents. The readers simply found it more difficult to function in the usual ways without their newspapers.

The newspaper reading habit, these researchers concluded, was a complex behavior, rooted in needs of the audience members. Understanding these needs was essential to understanding the way the audience entered into the communication contract implicit in the usual purchase of a newspaper.

The New York strike study is now somewhat dated, having been conducted before television was even on the scene, but the central findings remain unchallenged. The view of the active audience developed from the interview data has been supported by many studies of other media and other content.

Intensive interviews with habitual followers of daytime radio soap operas, for example, illustrated a relatively complex set of functions the messages were fulfilling for those listeners. Some who followed the serials, the study showed, sought emotional release from their own problems. They liked the unexpected developments in the programs, the sorrows of the characters, and the opportunities to release their own tensions through these removed crises. Others followed the serials because of the opportunities they provided for wishful thinking. The serials allowed audience members to compensate for deficiencies in their own lives. And a final reason people followed the serials, the researchers concluded, was to obtain advice. The programs taught appropriate patterns of behaviors, provided solutions to problems, offered explanations for human problems.

Recent research has shown that the reasons people have for attending to their newspapers, and to some extent, the public affairs programming of the broadcast media, can be grouped into six types. The most prominent reason, at least in the view of the audience members themselves, is for *surveillance* of the environment. In other words, many people feel they read a newspaper to learn what is going on in the world, to keep informed of events, to learn what is important and what they should know about.

Also of considerable importance, in the minds of the readers and viewers, is the information in the media that assists in day-to-day *decisions*. Well over half the readers, studies indicate, say the newspapers help them form opinions about things going on around them.

A third reason for using the media is to gain information useful in interpersonal *discussions*. Approximately a third of the readers, for example, say newspapers give them something to talk about with other people.

The media also allow some users to get the feeling they are actually *participating* in current events. In other words, they can live out some of their desires through the media.

read or which messages actually will be received. In fact, much of what we have discussed here suggests a great deal of overlap in perspectives. The discussion of communicatory utility, for example, has obvious overlap with the discussion of gratifications sought from the media. People seeking information from the media that will aid them in future communication are, to be sure, demonstrating the desire to receive useful information. There is redundancy in our discussion of research perspectives.

A general answer to the questions about relative influence of these forces on the active audience is not available. While researchers should feel concerned about this state of the art — and many clearly are — the practicing journalist can take some satisfaction in simply knowing that readers are very active participants in the communication process. Although we do not always know the reasons for the behavior, we know the audience behaves in relatively consistent ways, and we know its behavior must be entered into the communication equation. The practicing journalist who ignores the active role of the intended recipient is likely to do little real communicating.

5
Strangers, Friends, and Family

Each of us is a member of various social groups or categories, whether we want to be or not. By accidents of birth or fate, we can be classified according to a host of criteria. Each of us can be described in terms of age, sex, race or ethnic background, geographic origin, and social class, among others. Nothing we do ourselves can alter this classification much, at least in the short run. And whether we think it or not, we are in many respects similar to other people lumped into the same social *category* with us. People in such categories are not identical, to be sure, but they tend to be highly similar.

We also are members of various *social groups* over which we have a great deal of control. Most readers of this book will be college students, though no one really forced them into that category. Sure, their parents had some say, and economic realities entered into it. But they joined pretty much on their own. They also have selected, to a large degree, their social contacts on campus. They decided whether to join a fraternity or sorority, and which one to try to get into if they decided to do so. They decided whether to live on campus or off, whether to participate in intramural sports, whether to become active on the campus newspaper. In short, we put ourselves into lots of social groups. Voluntarily formed groups, as is true for involuntary ones, are most often highly homogeneous.

We use these groups, both involuntary and voluntary, frequently in daily conversation, which testifies to their validity. We describe friends in terms of their home towns and campus memberships. The pronouns *he* or *she* are implicit categorizations. They crop up everywhere.

Social scientists, too, have found such categorizations helpful. A good social category, from the point of view of the social scientist, is one that not only predicts, but also explains, behavior. Social categories can be used to predict the behavior of media audience members; some help to explain that behavior as well.

SOME INVOLUNTARY SOCIAL CATEGORIES

Some of us simply are better or worse off, socially speaking, than others. For a series of reasons, our occupations are valued more or less highly. Our life styles are thought to be superior or inferior. Our activities, more or less important. In other words, some of us have a higher social class than others. Social stratification often is quite arbitrary, or at least it can seem that way. Certainly there are arguments on both sides of any debate over whether college professors or sanitation workers are more important for society. But the former are afforded more status in this society (though sometimes paid less). The latter are left with little social standing. Many sanitation workers call themselves sanitation engineers, in acknowledgment of the higher status assigned people doing almost any kind of engineering, even if with waste products.

Social class makes a difference in human behavior patterns, as most of us know. People on the top do things people on the bottom don't. For one thing, people on the top are much more likely to read a daily newspaper. They are more likely to subscribe to magazines, particularly those dealing with public affairs, and they're more likely to watch public affairs programming on television. Because they are more likely to be media aficionados, they are more likely to be in your audience than are those on the bottom.

In part this stratification is explained by education. People of higher *socioeconomic status,* or *SES* to use the jargon of sociology, are usually better educated. Better educated people are more likely to be media users than are those with less education. But that isn't the whole picture. Higher SES people also are more likely to hold public affairs in high regard, to have internalized the norm that knowing what is going on, or at least appearing to know, is good for them, good for their social strivings, good for the future of democracy. In other words, it's a little like apple pie and motherhood. Lower SES people generally do like apple pie, but they see less value in keeping up on world events. It may simply be because they have less to say about them.

Age is another social category that makes a difference. Young adults are less likely to watch television news regularly, read a newspaper, or read magazines than are those in the middle-age groups. Generally, use of the public affairs content of the media increases at a regular rate until about retirement time, when the whole picture seems to change. But life styles change at that time, too, and health becomes a factor. So it isn't surprising to find that older people do less reading, both in newspapers and magazines. General television viewing is less affected by retirement. Studies show, as expected, that the actual number of hours in front of the set increases. Television news viewing, however, does seem to decrease after retirement.

Not only do young people use less of the public affairs media than their middle-aged counterparts, they also tend to consume different messages in the media. Young people, even those in the eighteen to twenty-four year old range, are more likely to read the comics page in the newspaper than are any of the elders. They are less likely to read any local news items, including those involving government, or to read items about international developments.

A study conducted in the early 1970s showed that the young were even less likely to read stories about Vietnam and related matters, despite the potential personal threat the war posed for them. Young people are more likely to read entertainment news, and about as likely to read about sports as are the older groups. Overall, the best bet, however, is that the older a person is, the more likely he or she will read all types of news stories.

Young people might be expected to be less frequent users of the public affairs media than their seniors for several reasons. Their lives are less settled, and they have less attachment to their community. There may be less social reward for being knowledgeable about world affairs. But the finding that young people are less interested in their newspapers than older people has only recently been documented so thoroughly. The possibility exists that a young cohort is being created that is not firmly tied to the news products. For journalism, of course, that poses a serious threat.

Another social category that affects media use habits is based on *sex*. Women are less likely to read stories in the daily newspaper about international affairs than are men but are as likely as men to read local news items and news about state and local government. Women, compared to men, read more horoscopes and work more puzzles, are less interested in environmental news and stories about labor problems, and are more interested in the obituaries, the television and radio logs, entertainment, letters to the editor, and human interest features in general. Men are more interested in business and finance news, sports, and political columns. Overall, however, the women are about as likely to read the average news item as men. In other words, the sex differences tend to balance out when the whole paper is considered. Women are as likely to read a newspaper on a given day as men. They spend about the same amount of time with the paper.

The differences that do exist between the sexes are not hard to explain. Women traditionally have been assigned a different role in our society than men, and as a consequence, are likely to find different kinds of messages of value to them. Labor news is probably of more interest to the principal wage earner of a household, who traditionally has been a man. That picture is changing, of course, and the media habits of men and women are likely to become more similar as the roles of the two sexes become more similar. The advent of magazines such as *Ms.* suggests just such a trend. They provide information for women that the other media were ignoring.

Another social category that can affect communication is *race*. In general, blacks have been found to use the broadcast media more and depend on those media more for news and entertainment than do whites. But the picture is clouded somewhat by the strong relationship between race and social class. Black people are more likely to be in the lower SES groups. And as we have seen, considerable differences in media use habits exist between lower and higher SES groups.

A study conducted in the late 1960s in Lansing, Michigan, shows that low income whites and blacks are relatively similar in media use habits, but both groups differ significantly from higher SES groups. The researchers found low income whites and blacks spent about the same amount of time viewing television on an average day (over half of each group watched four or more hours). But both groups spent considerably more time with that medium than did the population at large (only one in five had watched four or more hours). Low income whites and blacks also were similar in terms of the number of hours they listened to radio, the frequency of magazine readership, and how often they attended movies. The blacks were considerably heavier users of the phonograph. Blacks reported owning more records and listening to them more often.

Low income blacks also were less likely to subscribe to a daily newspaper than were low income whites. Both groups subscribed less frequently than the population at large. Among low SES whites, about one in four reported regularly reading all of the paper. Among low SES blacks, only one in ten reported that behavior. In terms of actual pages read within the paper, however, no differences existed between the two groups.

When asked which of the media they preferred for local news, low income blacks and low income whites showed about equal acceptance of television, with about three out of ten picking that medium. But the blacks were more likely to reject all of the media and opt for ''other people'' as the source for their news than were the low SES whites. Newspapers tended to be slightly more popular with the whites than the blacks.

These findings suggest some real differences do exist between the racial groups, while other apparent differences are due simply to differences in socioeconomic status. The differences not attributable to SES, of course, are due to other variations in the experiences of the racial groups. While some of those differences can be expected to decrease in the future, there is some evidence of a countervailing trend.

Studies of low income black and low income white children in East Cleveland, Ohio, and in Philadelphia have shown that children in the two racial groups tend to be quite different in their media habits. These black grade and high school students were found to watch more television than their white counterparts (despite the Lansing finding that adults differed little) and to express more belief in the reality of television content.

The children may become more like the adults as they get older, and the differences between the racial groups may fade. Or, adult members of the two racial groups may be less accepting in the future of the messages from the print media. The possibility of the second trend, coupled with the possibility that newspaper reading among young people in general is continuing to decline, has serious implications for journalism.

FAMILY BACKGROUND

Family membership shares something with both the involuntary group membership discussed so far and the voluntary ones to follow. As is true for involuntary groups, members of families have little control over membership. To be sure, parents choose each other. The offspring do not. And the offspring are of most concern to us here. But in contrast to the categories of social class, age, sex, and race, there is a high degree of contact among family members. In that way, families are much more like peer groups or other voluntary social groups that form throughout life.

The *family* is the dominant mechanism by which our society transmits its values to new members. It can be rivaled in terms of impact only by the educational system. Since the family has control over the child during some of the most formative years, most psychologists and sociologists say it is the major influence.

The family is the primary tool for teaching gross motor activities such as walking, for providing the raw materials central to language acquisition, and for instruction in all sorts of cultural and moral values. It isn't surprising, then, that the family setting is also an important one for learning about the news media. In fact, many of the differences between the SES, sexual, and racial groups we've noted probably result from influences of the family.

The relationship between parent and child media use patterns, however, isn't necessarily straightforward. Several studies do show, for example, significant relationships between adolescent and parental use of television, with parents and children watching roughly the same amount of television and kinds of shows. While some researchers attribute this to a modeling phenomenon, whereby the children simply do what they see their parents do, there is some evidence this is not the case. Instead, it seems, *parents* at least sometimes do what their *children* do, following program suggestions made by the children or giving in to the children when family interests do not mesh.

One study of adolescents has shown, for example, that regardless of the type of television program under consideration, about four out of ten parents said that the child had selected or recommended the broadcast. Another study found more instances of parents asking their high school children for program advice than vice versa. And regardless of the direction of any modeling, there also is evidence of dissimilarities between how children and parents use media. At least one study, for example, has found no evidence that young males either model or influence the book reading of their parents.

Parents may influence the media use habits of their children in a less direct way, however. This influence seems to result not so much from modeling specific behaviors, but rather from the learning of styles of communicatory behavior in the home. A study of over 1200 families in five Wisconsin communities by Chaffee, McLeod, and Atkin, for example, has shown only mild relationships between the amount of time parents and junior and senior high school students spend watching television in general, viewing news programming, and reading newspapers. But the study did show that those parents who taught their children *styles of interpersonal communication* that required large amounts of information on public affairs were more likely than other parents to have children who read the newspapers and paid particular atttention to public affairs programming on television. Evidence of modeling by the child of parental media use habits occurred only in those families placing high value on social relationships conducive to such patterning.

This Wisconsin study is worth elaborating on briefly because it provides a groundwork for the discussion to follow on the interface between mass communication and interpersonal factors. These data and numerous other studies suggest there are at least two styles of communication that parents can and often do teach their children. The first style, which has been labeled *socio-orientation,* stresses the importance of maintaining harmonious personal relations, avoiding controversy, and repressing personal feeling. The second style, which has been called *concept-orientation,* stresses the importance for the child of expressing his or her own ideas, using conversation to discuss controversy, and challenging positions taken by parents and others. Parents can stress either of these styles of communications, neither of them, or both of them.

Families that stress neither have been labeled *laissez-faire.* Children are not prohibited from challenging parents' views, but neither are they encouraged to do so. Children in these families, it seems, are given few directions on the use of interpersonal communications.

Families stressing the social relations exclusively have been called *protective.* The child is encouraged to get along with others, taught not to confront or express dissent, and given little chance to encounter discrepant information. These children are given a clear directive: use interpersonal communications to keep peace.

Pluralistic families are those emphasizing concept-oriented communication independent of the consequences such communication may have on social relations. The children are told: ideas are important. Form opinions and discuss them openly.

The *consensual* families are perhaps the most complex. The child is given apparently conflicting signals to maintain social harmony through communication, yet told to introduce diverse points of view in conversations. In other words, these children are told to keep the peace *while* expressing strong opinions.

The consequences of these styles of communication, presented schematically in figure 5.1, were clear in the Wisconsin study discussed above. They determined to a considerable degree the media habits of the children. In fact, these communication styles taught in the home have been found to affect a wide range of childhood behaviors. Children from *pluralistic* homes, for example, have been found to be more knowledgeable about public affairs, earn better grades in school, be more active in school and politics, and want to be more like their parents. *Protective* children spend little time with school homework and make low grades in high school, spend little time in extracurricular political activities, and are moderate in terms of political knowledge.

Consensual children are low in political knowledge, spend lots of time with homework but get only moderate grades, and are only moderately active in political matters. The *laissez-faire* families have children who spend little time on homework and earn moderate grades, spend little time in political activity, and are moderately knowledgeable about politics.

The *consensual* children, and those from *protective* homes, have been found to watch high amounts of violence on television. The *laissez-faire* children watch moderate amounts, while the *pluralistic* are very low in terms of violence viewing.

This research on family communication patterns reinforces the notion that mass communication does not exist in a vacuum. Rather, the message is re-

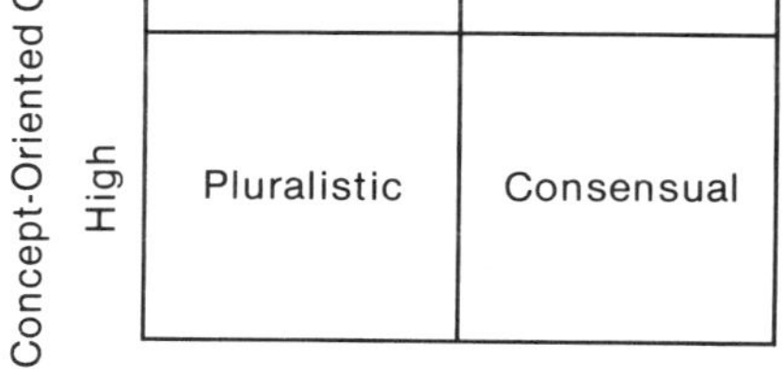

Fig. 5.1 Family Communication Types

ceived in and moderated by the social environment in which audience members find themselves. To restate our theme, the social environment of each audience member poses potential barriers to communication between the professional mass communicator and those for whom the message is designed.

THE INTERPERSONAL ENVIRONMENT

The Columbia University sociologists who undertook the classic 1940 study of voters in Erie County, Ohio, expected to find that political information conveyed by the mass media affected the outcome of the campaign. For a number of reasons, including the discovery of selective exposure patterns, they soon changed their position. The media, they concluded, served more to reinforce positions than to change them.

This conclusion was based to a large degree on what the respondents had told the Columbia researchers. Those interviewed said that *interpersonal contacts* were more important to them than the media in deciding how to vote. Based on this and other evidence, the Columbia researchers concluded that there existed a *two-step flow* of communication in our society. Messages entered the social environment of a community through *opinion leaders,* who received the messages from the media and in turn passed them on to those followers inclined to discuss matters of public importance. Opinion leaders were thought to be the key to understanding the dynamics of change in any campaign setting.

While many of these early conclusions have been challenged, especially those about the very limited effects of mass media, considerable evidence has been amassed about the importance of social networks in understanding media effects. Opinion leaders, those persons who said they tried to convince someone else of their political views and had been asked for advice on politics, were found in the Erie County study to be more interested in the political campaign and to claim greater exposure to the mass media. In fact, even after removing the influence of interest, opinion leaders were found to be higher in media use during the campaign than others in the population. In other words, those who said they tried to influence votes and had been regularly asked their opinion were the ones who followed the campaign extensively in the media. Those who didn't try to persuade and weren't contacted used the news media less.

A general relationship between media use and interpersonal discussion has been amply demonstrated in a host of settings. After the Nixon-Kennedy debates in the 1960 presidential campaign, for example, one study found that 56 percent of the viewers of the debate also reported having conversations about it. There was considerable selectivity, however, in that discussion. Of those who talked about the debate, almost half reported their communication partners shared the same views. About two out of five of those who talked about the debate did so both with some individuals who agreed with them and others who did not. Only one in ten reported talking about the debate only with people holding views unlike their own.

Consistent with the two-step flow notion, those who were high media users in general (regular readers of the newspapers and users of the broadcast media) were more likely to have talked about the debate than those who used the media less. In fact, those who either watched the first debate on television or heard it on radio *and* read about it in the paper were the people who did the most talking about that encounter between the two candidates. Those who were exposed to the debate via the radio or television broadcast *or* read about it were ranked second in terms of subsequent discussion of the debate. Those who talked least were the ones who had not been exposed at all.

While these findings support the idea that the media's messages are transmitted through the community secondhand by the persons who get them directly, only 4 percent of those studied—about one in twenty-five persons— reported hearing about the debate through conversation alone. When the media are so pervasive and enough warning has been given of the event, few people get all of their information via interpersonal sources.

The relationship between interpersonal discussion and reception of mass communicated messages is probably more complex than the two-step flow notion suggests. It almost certainly is of a cyclical nature. In other words, reading a newspaper account of an event such as the first of the so-called 1960 Great Debates probably did stimulate people to later discuss that event, but previous discussion of politics probably led many people to read the account or actually tune in to the debate in the first place. The discussion of the first debate probably stimulated people to view the second or parts of the subsequent debates. That viewing may have led to further discussion. The same pattern no doubt held for the 1976 debates between Gerald Ford and Jimmy Carter as well as other events like it.

While much of the research on the link between interpersonal and mass communication follows the two-step flow model and regards mass communication as directing the focus of interpersonal conversations, a number of studies have looked at how personal conversations influence the use of mass media. Table 5.1 shows this influence on readership of articles in a church magazine by both clergy and laymen. There we see that the number of conversations during the past month is strongly related to whether any articles were read on the contemporary social role of the church. While it is impossible to determine from the data which come first—the discussions or the reading—it is clear that the two behaviors are strongly linked empirically. The number of conversations is an excellent predictor of reading.

The cyclical relationship between interpersonal communication and media use cropped up in our discussion of informational utility in chapter 4. Those

Table 5.1 Percentage of Persons Reading Magazine Articles on the Contemporary Social Role of the Church*

	Read Any Articles During Past Month?	
Number of Conversations on Topic During Past Month	Percent Answering No	Percent Answering Yes
None (n = 44)	95.5	4.5
One or Two (n = 62)	51.6	48.4
Three or More (n = 53)	20.8	79.2

* Adapted from Jacqueline J. Harris and Maxwell E. McCombs, "The Interpersonal/Mass Communication Interface Among Church Leaders," *Journal of Communication,* 22, no. 3 (1972), 261. Reprinted by permission of the International Communication Association.

stories or news items perceived as potentially useful in the future, we noted, are more likely to be read or viewed. Often utility is determined by the social setting. People who think they will use a particular piece of information in a future conversation attend to that message. People in social settings offering such communicatory opportunities are more likely to perceive the utility of the information.

This cyclical relationship is illustrated also by a study of the role of pop music for English secondary school children. Researchers found that both involvement in and knowledge about the intricacies of pop music played an integral role in the social groups formed within these schools. Those students best in naming songs currently on the Top Ten charts were found to be the same students mentioned by other students as friends.

Students seemed to be sensitive to the importance of pop music knowledge, able to say which students were most knowledgeable on the topics, and took that information into account when evaluating the other students. Indirect evidence suggests, in addition, that those students who already were most knowledgeable about the music were likely to want to know more about such music in the future. The popular students were the most interested in the topic in general—the knowledge about music, after all, helped make them popular because the students talked about pop music often. And the recognition of this fact led the popular students to seek more information about pop music in the future, perhaps to maintain the position they had earned.

In addition to stimulating media use directly, the social setting probably has indirect influences paralleling those we have seen in the family. Many social groups have norms that affect media use in much the way family communication styles stimulate or restrict media use of children. Some social groups seem to thrive on controversy and have communicative directives similar to those in the pluralistic families. For such groups, the introduction of diverse points of view seems to be essential. Members of such groups are expected to be frequent media users to obtain fuel for the discussions.

Other social groups, more like the protective families, frown on controversy, stress the importance of social harmony, and do not reward open discussion. Members of such groups, in contrast, are not expected to be heavy media users. Many political discussion groups and cooperatives that developed in the period of campus turmoil of the late 1960s clearly followed the former model. Campus fraternities and sororities during that same era seemed to be more inclined toward the latter.

To sum up, the social setting imposes some important barriers on the professional communicator. Some of the barriers discussed in this chapter are new, while others have surfaced in somewhat different forms in our earlier discussions in chapter 2, 3, and 4. In our previous discussion our focus was on the individual as information processor; here our discussion focused on the social environment in which the processing takes place. Together these discussions present a comprehensive view of the audience to which the mediated message is directed.

PART TWO
THE
COMMUNICATOR

6
The Communicator's Social Base of Operation

To this point in our behavior stylebook, we have given attention almost exclusively to the communication barriers erected by audiences of the mass media. The implicit assumption has been that the professional communicator and his or her organization have behaved flawlessly and that the technology used for distribution of the messages was finely tuned. It is an assumption we feel very uncomfortable with, but one that has served our purposes very well up to this point.

From one perspective, the behavior of the professional communicator isn't very important in determining if communication has taken place. One simply examines the message produced by the communicator and then decides if the audience member received the message and understood its content. That perspective, however, is unsatisfactory for a journalist because, for the most part, the journalist isn't concerned with the message *per se*. Rather, the journalist is concerned with the message as a representation of some aspect of the environment. The message is meant to reflect some objective reality.

A printed or broadcast news story about a fire isn't the fire itself, but it is designed to portray in some symbolic form what the fire was. The reader who didn't witness the fire will feel the realities of being there. If that doesn't happen, the professional communicator has failed.

It is easy to blame the reader for such failures. We have already shown how readers don't always read what they should. Sometimes they read only what suits their views of things. Sometimes they read only what will make them look good to their friends. Sometimes they distort what they do read.

The professional communicator, nevertheless, has a lot to say about the success of the communication. The members of the audience shouldn't be left with all the blame. In many regards, since the professional has taken it upon himself or herself to initiate the "conversation," much of the burden rests with the journalist. "While it takes two to communicate," the audience member can always say, "you're the one who initiated this encounter. And it's your job to communicate."

SOME ROLES
PROFESSIONAL COMMUNICATORS
PLAY

Mass media messages are a group product. First there's the reporter, who has firsthand contact with the raw materials of the story. Most often, the reporter also writes the story. But sometimes he or she gets help from someone on the desk; particularly with breaking stories, the reporter telephones a rewrite specialist who does most of the message assembly.

Even when the reporter does the writing, it usually passes through the hands, and under the pencil, of at least one editor. The editor's jobs are many. One of the most important is to improve the message so that it gets read.

Many desk people are really news managers, too, or work directly under managers. These news managers make decisions affecting the stories reporters work on and the information they gather. In other words, they shape the stories even before the editing process begins. They assign the stories, influence what the reporter puts in the stories, then edit the stories after they are written. No other single person has so much influence on message production.

After the message leaves the hands of the editors and news managers, it goes to the technicians. The role of the technician is to connect the reporter to the audience. In the newspaper and magazine industry, the printers and assorted craftsmen are the key technicians, though their role has been diminished by the advent of the computerized newsroom. In the broadcast field these technicians are the assortment of directors, camera people, and engineers responsible for getting the message onto the airwaves.

There are, then, at least four groups of people who have some *input* to any given message. The reporters who gather the information we might call information *collectors*. The *information processors* are those writers and editors who concentrate on the stylistic aspects of the message. The city editors and upper level administrators are *news managers*. The final group is made up of the *technicians*.

The larger the news organization, the more differentiated these groups and their roles are likely to be. Some very small operations may combine the four, but such operations largely are a thing of the past, for they fail to offer the strengths needed for organizational survival in today's complex society. Large media operations even differentiate within these groups. In a typical large newsroom, for example, the information processors might be of several types. One group might concentrate on city news. Another might handle only state copy. Yet another might handle national and international affairs. The information collectors—the reporters—might also be so differentiated. Such subgroups are intended to improve organizational performance, which is measured, at least in part, in terms of message production.

The information collector/processor distinction merits additional elaboration. In general, journalists are unaccustomed to thinking in such terms, preferring instead to see the tasks of information gatherer and information processor as the same. The talents required for the two tasks, however, are quite distinct. The latter is essentially a stylistic operation involving the manipulation of symbols. Good writers are those who produce stylistically superior messages. Information gathering involves other talents, such as persistence and unchecked curiosity. A good reporter is one who never stops asking ''Why?''

What makes the content of a newspaper or news broadcast different from fiction is the information in those messages. Fiction and news require good writing. Of the two, only news work requires reporting.

Jack Anderson, considered by some to be a prototypical investigative reporter, is not an outstanding writer. His columns work because of the information in them, not because of the style of presentation. The Watergate team of Bob Woodward and Carl Bernstein, the reporters who did much of the *Washington Post's* investigation of the Watergate scandal, also illustrates this split. As shown in their book and film, *All the President's Men,* each half of Woodstein, as they often are called, represented a particular competence in the writer and reporter roles. Woodward had a reputation as a smooth, competent investigator who had difficulties with his writing. Bernstein, whose reporting habits sometimes gave him and his editors problems, was a smooth, competent writer. Together, Woodward and Bernstein were a success.

Students shouldn't console themselves with good writing and bad reporting, or the reverse. The examples, instead, are offered to illustrate the realities of the news operation. Writing and reporting require separate talents, but the good journalist has both. Woodward and Bernstein, after all, held down good jobs before they benefited from their team relationship.

THE JOURNALIST'S BAGGAGE

In their roles as writers and reporters, professionals come under various influences that affect their performance. Some of these influences are built into the job. Others are not. All affect the message produced and, therefore, the communication process.

In much the same way that individual audience members select from the available messages, each reporter selects from the information before him or her each day and presents only fragments of that information to the news editors and managers. The editors and managers further reduce the range of the message by deciding to use some stories and not others and by deciding to present some stories in more conspicuous places than others.

This process can be viewed as a gradual funneling of information from the environment, which sits at the most open end of the funnel, to the audience members, who are at the funnel's mouth. The *background, capabilities, training,* and *values* that the gatherers, processors, and managers bring to the news-gathering and message production phases of the communication process very much affect the selectivity that goes into it.

Journalists are a pretty atypical lot, all things considered. According to a 1971 national survey of journalists, conducted by sociologists John Johnstone, Edward Slawski, and William Bowman, about half come from professional or managerial families. Journalists are overwhelmingly male, overwhelmingly white, and fairly well educated. Most completed college and almost one in five has done advanced degree work.

This kind of *background,* of course, can create problems of perspective. People tend to see things in terms they know and understand from past experiences. The experiences of the professional journalist are not those of a large number of people in the population. While former Vice President Spiro Agnew's charge that the media in the United States are part of an elite Eastern Establishment is open to serious question, there is little doubt the press forms an elite very different from much of the population. Many press critics, particularly those from subcultures in the society, feel that establishment journalists, as the elite are often called, do not have the ability or desire to empathize with the nonelite.

The National Advisory Commission on Civil Disorders, formed by President Lyndon Johnson to investigate the causes of the 1967 racial riots, wrote succinctly:

> The media report and write from the standpoint of a white man's world. The ills of the ghetto, the difficulties of life there, the Negro's burning sense of grievance, are seldom conveyed. Slights and indignities are part of the Negro's daily life, and many of them come from what he now calls "the white press"—a press that repeatedly, if unconsciously, reflects the biases, the paternalism, the indifference of white America. This may be understandable, but it is not excusable in an institution that has the mission to inform and educate the whole of our society.*

* National Advisory Commission on Civil Disorders, *Report of the Commission* (New York: Bantam, 1968), p. 366.

There is evidence journalism is taking steps to remedy this situation. News organizations have made significant efforts to recruit blacks and other minorities into the profession. The number of minority training programs and fellowships offered by journalism schools and departments has increased. Women, as well, are becoming more sought after by news organizations. Until the backgrounds of journalists match to a considerable degree those of various audience members, those backgrounds present potential problems.

The *intellectual capabilities* of journalists, independent of their social background, also are important influences on the news operation. Via the educational system, the journalism profession creates an intellectual elite who are employed as gatherers and processors. The activities of a journalist are intellectually challenging, requiring speed of thought and systematic assimilation of information. Only those who survive the educational system, obtain at least a college degree, and can pass screening employment exams are considered capable of such performance. Some organizations still hire journalists without college degrees, but they are few and will decrease in number even further as more degrees are granted yearly by the journalism schools across the country.

A reporter incapable of almost instantaneous analysis of information, sifting of materials, and processing of what might to others seem insignificant data, will produce a different message than the more capable reporter. Inattention to detail decreases the information that can be transmitted to the audience and allows for possible distortion in the message.

Journalism *training* is designed to make reporters as equal as possible in terms of such things as observational competence and experience in handling both simple and difficult assignments. For the most part, such training does establish some bottom line of competence. Journalism majors know at least the basics of writing and reporting. Because journalism programs also focus on the liberal arts and the social sciences, most journalism graduates have something of a generalist's training as well. But great inequalities of training remain. The student who works hardest, gains experience both in and outside of the classroom, and pushes himself or herself the most, makes the best reporter. Such a reporter, in all probability, will produce the account of an event most approximating the event itself. The untrained or inexperienced reporter will miss important details, and the result is a distorted collection of information about that event or situation.

Particularly in large news organizations, considerable specialization is taking place in news assignments. Persons specially trained in law are being hired to do legal reporting. Those who have taken courses in biology and related fields are being hired to do environmental reporting. Students with some training in agriculture are given preference for the farm beat. Many journalism schools are now developing special training programs at the graduate level to educate students in these and other specialties. The popularity of these pro-

Table 6.1 Ratings of Various Occupations*

	Percent Rating People in Profession "Very High" or "High" in Terms of Honesty and Ethical Standards
Medical Doctors	56
Engineers	49
College Teachers	44
Journalists	*33*
Lawyers	25
Building Contractors	23
Business Executives	20
Senators	19
Congressmen	14
Labor Union Leaders	12
Advertising Practitioners	11

* Adapted from *The Gallup Opinion Index,* 134 (September 1976), 17. Reprinted by permission.

decisions, such as the Pentagon Papers ruling against prior restraint of the press, have strengthened the legal protection of the journalism profession.

It is the degree to which journalists hold values typical of other professionals that is often in question. Discussed less, but of equal importance, is the extent to which the actual work setting of journalists encourages professional conduct. Persons in professions generally place much value on such things as autonomy in carrying out work tasks, individual opportunities for public service, and freedom from supervision. Work settings in the true professions encourage autonomy, public service, and freedom from supervision.

One study, conducted in Milwaukee, Wisconsin, showed considerable acceptance of professional values by working journalists. Three out of four of the journalists studied, for example, said they thought the ideal job was one that allowed for originality and initiative, a characteristic of the established professions. Two out of five said they thought it important to have a job that offered an opportunity to influence the public's thinking. By and large, however, the journalists did not think their present employment situation provided them with the professional satisfaction they desired. The jobs did provide them with satisfaction in nonprofessional areas such as job security, social harmony, and indications of self-importance.

Discussions about the professional standing of journalism can be dismissed as moot unless it is demonstrated that such standing is related to the way the job actually is carried out. If a journalist does a good job of gathering and transmitting information, what difference does it make whether he or she is a member of the profession?

Studies do indicate, however, an important relationship between the professional attitudes of journalists and the way their newspapers perform. One study, for example, found that photojournalists with professional attitudes were most likely to be working for newspapers considered by experts to be good in terms of visual communications. Journalists lacking these professional attitudes worked for the weaker papers.

This finding was replicated in a second study dealing with general newspaper performance. Again, the better papers were the ones with reporters and editors holding professional values. In addition, the better papers provided working conditions more supportive of professional ethics. When the two forces were considered together, it was found that working conditions, rather than the attitudes of the staffers, was the more important correlate of performance.

NEWSROOM PRESSURES

The journalist doesn't work in a social vacuum, of course, but rather in a complex social situation. At the bottom of the journalism hierarchy are the information gatherers and low-level processors. In the United States, roughly three out of four of the approximately 70,000 full-time journalists working in the news media fall into these lower categories. The next group of professionals is the news managers who determine day-to-day policy within certain broad guidelines and see to it that this policy is carried out. At the top of the hierarchy is the owner, publisher, or corporate head of the news operation. The person at the top determines basic policy.

All news operations have *policy,* defined as the more or less consistent orientations shown by a paper regarding selected issues and events. These orientations are expressed in general guidelines on how news is to be handled, particularly news of interest to the publishers. These generally are positive guidelines. Equal coverage of racial groups is one such policy of most newspapers. Negative policies often have to do with coverage of "sacred cows" — those persons or groups given preferential treatment regardless of activity. It is important to note that these policies are seldom spelled out formally within a news operation. Rather, they are transmitted in subtle ways that tell much about the actual news operation and process of communication.

Sociologist Warren Breed, in a classic study of journalists and news operations, identified some of the ways staffers come to learn the policy of their news operation. Since most staffers read the newspaper they produce, and many are openly required to do so, they learn a great deal about the product through observation of what is normally used and how it is played—in other words, what the newspaper is *supposed* to look like.

But the staffer also gets feedback on the particular copy he or she has produced, and this feedback helps further to establish policy. If certain kinds of stories are edited heavily, cut in length, or simply not run, the reporter learns that some policy probably exists regarding those stories. Conversely, reporters receive positive feedback in the form of prominent display of stories and favorable comments from the editors. This positive feedback serves as a reward for following policy.

Reporters and editors also learn much about their chief executives by simply observing them in the newsroom, by knowing what they do in their free time, by knowing where they live, and by reading their comments when they appear in internal memoranda or "house organs." If the publisher lunches frequently with the chairman of the local chamber of commerce, entertains local business executives, and chats personally about local community leaders, he or she is revealing important things about newspaper policy.

Breed discovered several reasons why staffers follow the policy of their newspaper once they have learned it. The first is obvious: though actual dismissals are not common in the industry, people do fear them. Lack of promotion or actual demotion are lesser, though important, sanctions used by the publishers. Many staffers fall in line because they aspire to higher positions.

Other reasons, however, include the generally congenial relationships that exist in the newsroom, where all members are viewed as part of the team. Editors seldom treat reporters as true underlings, often instead deferring to the judgment of the writer or reporter. Most reporters like their jobs, and the congenial relationships help to make the policies of the paper acceptable. In other words, the newsroom itself provides *social support* for acceptance of policy.

The policy, of course, does not always contradict what the reporter actually believes is correct. Policy can be aggressiveness in the pursuit of those kinds of news that staffers find quite acceptable.

A large number of situations, Breed discovered, allow for deviation from the newspaper's policy. Reporters and editors are sometimes able to circumvent policy or actually contradict it directly, partly because policy isn't always definitive, and it isn't always clear that the behavior of the staffer actually violates that policy.

The staffer gains considerable latitude, as well, by nature of the work he or she does. Because executives are often ignorant of the details of a given story, the reporter or person who did the information gathering is in a position of some authority. The news managers must take the staffer's view of the situation, particularly when deadlines approach and alternative perspectives are difficult to obtain.

The *star system* within the newsroom also provides situations where policy can be broken. Certain reporters develop status within the journalistic and general community that gives them power to negotiate with and even make demands of their hierarchical superiors. The perspectives and interpretations of certain columnists and political reporters, even if not in mesh with those of the owners, often get into the paper simply because the star's following carries some weight. Beginning, or cub, reporters, of course, have great difficulty pulling this off. Any imbalance in the job market resulting in an oversupply of eager young reporters only aggravates the weak standing of the beginning staffers.

Breed's analysis of the newsroom emphasizes a *conflict model* of behavior, but there is evidence this model doesn't apply in a great many newsrooms. Most newspapers have a reputation, and persons applying for jobs with these papers are aware of it. As a consequence, a fair amount of selectivity by applicants leads to conformity, not conflict.

It is unlikely, for example, that many persons apply for jobs at the Manchester, New Hampshire, *Union Leader* without being aware of the conservative politics of publisher William Loeb. Loeb's job becomes easier, since much of the selective recruitment and rigorous socialization his editors otherwise might have to undertake is unnecessary. His paper's reputation has taken care of that for him.

It is possible to get a good idea of just how often publishers involve themselves directly in the news decision process from a national study conducted by David R. Bowers. In order to find out more about the publisher–managing editor relationship, Bowers sent questionnaires to evening newspapers (which outnumber morning papers by more than four to one) across the country.

About half of the managing editors said their publishers never gave them directives or suggestions about use of copy, specific information to be included or excluded, or display of the copy in the paper. But the answers weren't uniform across all kinds of stories. Specifically, the editors said publishers exercised most influence on local copy, followed by state and regional copy, national copy, and then foreign and international news. In other words, the closer to home the story, the more likely publishers were to have a hand in how it was used.

Table 6.2 shows the general pattern. The publishers were more likely to

Table 6.2 Percentage of Publishers Directing Editorial Decisions of Editors for Various Kinds of Stories*

	Percentage Directing Decisions
Local Stories	65
State, Regional Stories	48
National Stories	39
International Stories	34

* Adapted from David R. Bowers, "A Report on Activity by Publishers in Directing Newsroom Decisions," *Journalism, Quarterly,* 44 (1967), 45. Reprinted by permission.

interfere when the copy affected them personally or was likely to affect the financial well-being of the paper than when it did not. Almost half of the managing editors said their publishers at least occasionally issued directives or gave advice when the image of the local community was involved. About one in three of the editors said their publishers got involved at least occasionally in stories about the paper itself or its employees, and an equal number said the publisher at least occasionally had input on stories about major or important advertisers. Only about one in five of the editors, however, said the publishers interfered with copy on local labor relations. For national stories on labor relations, the proportion was one in ten.

When publishers do get involved in the handling of stories, they are more likely to attempt to affect content and display than whether the story is actually used. And overall, the larger the circulation of the newspaper, the less active the publisher is likely to be in news direction. As we noted earlier, larger papers are more differentiated in terms of role. Publishers on such papers cannot easily involve themselves in day-to-day decisions on news operations and still perform their other tasks. This doesn't necessarily mean, of course, that the publisher has no influence on the operations of the larger papers; the influence may simply be more indirect.

Since even on the smallest papers, the publisher cannot be present for all decisions, other staff members have important influences on individual behavior in the newsroom. As Breed's analysis indicated, the colleagual contacts within the newroom are often essential in passing on the policy of the paper. But fellow staffers are important in yet another way: they help beginning reporters and editors *define reality* in ways that have little direct bearing on the newspaper policy.

Any given news situation is complex, entailing much information on diverse aspects of the event. The reporter has to select from that situation what is important. And the reporter has to give some meaning to the event, or put the pieces together so they represent the reality rather than an unconnected string of data. In many cases, however, the meaning of the observed phenomena isn't clear. There may be several possible interpretations, and it is difficult to determine which is correct—or even most likely to be correct. In such cases, it seems, reporters often rely on each other to determine just what it all means.

Timothy Crouse, reporter for *Rolling Stone* magazine, watched this process of journalistic interdependence while covering the 1972 campaign of Richard Nixon and George McGovern. Crouse later wrote a book about press coverage of the campaign, calling much of what he saw *pack journalism*. One incident reported in his book helps illustrate the role of colleagues in sorting out some of the complexities of the campaign. It details how reporters relied on the *New York Times'* national political reporter, R. W. "Johnny" Apple, Jr., for guidance when covering the Iowa Democratic caucuses of 1972. Apple is one of those labeled as a *media heavy* by Crouse. Here's why!

The Iowa precinct caucuses were the first test of [Sen. Edmund] Muskie's strength and thirty or forty reporters—national political reporters, campaign reporters, men from small papers—descended on Des Moines to report and interpret the results. When they crowded into the tiny, steamy Democratic headquarters on the night of January 24 to hear a local Democratic official announce the hour-by-hour returns, none of them could make much sense of the figures. Except for Apple.

A McGovern worker who was present recalled the scene. It was the first time he had ever seen the national press in operation. "It really amazed me," he said, "because what happened was that Johnny Apple . . . sat in a corner and everyone peered over his shoulder to find out what he was writing. The AP guy was looking over one shoulder, the UPI guy over the other and CBS, NBC, ABC and the Baltimore *Sun* were all crowding in behind. See, it wasn't like a primary. No one knew how to interpret these figures, nobody knew what was good and what was bad, so they were all taking it off Apple. He would sit down and write a lead, and they would go write leads. Then he'd change his lead when more results came in, and they'd all change theirs accordingly. When he wanted quiet to hear the guy announce the latest returns, he'd shout for quiet and they'd all shut up. Finally, at midnight, the guy announced that Muskie had 32 percent and McGovern had 26 percent, and Apple sat down to write his final story. He called it something like a surprisingly strong showing for George McGovern. Everyone peered over his shoulder again and picked it up. It was on the front page of every major newspaper the next day.*

While the complexities of the national political scene and the Iowa system of electing delegates to the convention probably exaggerated the interdependence of the reporters, other situations have illustrated the process as well. Reporters can help each other determine what is important in any given situation. Through acceptance of some common norms, the reporters focus on the same aspects of the story, using the same guides for what the story is all about.

On the whole, of course, there is a great deal of competition among working journalists. Even within the same newsroom, journalists often compete with each other for good stories. In the early days of Watergate, reporters Woodward and Bernstein often found themselves working against each other rather than together. It took the efforts of good editors as well as the recognition of mutual benefit on the part of both reporters to mold the reporting team.

But even in competitive situations reporters reinforce each other. They often share a common view of reality, which narrows down the events of the world by excluding those aspects of reality that do not fit the reportorial definition. Reporters themselves shape the reality on which the communication message is based.

---

* Timothy Crouse, *The Boys on the Bus* (New York: Ballatine, 1973), pp. 84–85. Reprinted by permission of Random House, Inc.

7
What's News?

In general, mass communicators do share a common definition of what is news. It is what's important. It's current. It's exciting. It's unusual. It's what is going on in the world around them. The basis for this common definition of news is occupational training and experience. News judgment is learned in college and reinforced on the job. New practices are transmitted through the social structure of the news organization from the most experienced person to the least. Even across news media, there is some consensus as to what is and what is not news. The generally well documented similarities of the news coverage of media across the country support this observation. On any given day, the front pages of the nation's papers will differ to some degree. Across time, however, papers give a surprisingly similar amount of space to news of the same general types.

NEWS DEFINITIONS

This consistency of news judgments over time is illustrated well by a study of the editorial content of six upstate New York newspapers in 1950 and 1970. The study examined the news and feature stories on the front pages of the newspapers, classifying each piece of copy into one of the fifteen categories listed in table 7.1. Despite the drastic changes that had taken place in society during the twenty-year span of the study, none of the fifteen news categories recorded a change of more than four percentage points. Reporters, editors, and publishers continued producing a highly similar product over an entire generation.

Model 1

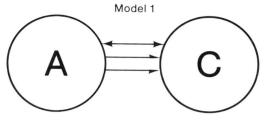

The communication acts of the two communicators, A and C, respectively, take place within frames of reference (the circles), separated by well-differentiated bureaucratic functions, role assignments and perceptions, social distance, values, etc. The flow of information in channels (double line) tends to be formal. The extra-message communications channel (single line) also is formal and is likely to be used when a message is in the main channel.

Model 2

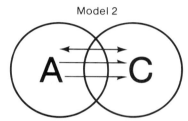

The frame of reference of A and C overlap; the two communicators cooperate in achieving their communication roles and, in part, share the values underlying the communications roles and acts. The flow of information occurs in an informal setting and the extra-channel messages are profuse.

Model 3

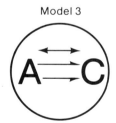

The frame of reference for one communicator has been absorbed or otherwise taken over by the other; there is no distinction in role perception and values. The communication act of one communicator is the cue to the other. The flow of information in the message channel is gauged by the extra-message discourse.

Fig. 7.1 Models of Relationships between Source *(A)* and Reporter *(C)* (Adapted from Walter Gieber and Walter Johnson, "The City Hall 'Beat': A Study of Reporter and Source Roles," *Journalism Quarterly,* 38 [1961], 290–91. Reprinted by permission.)

News → potential to influence other narratives
documentary - controversy - often makes news
seizing of tapes etc

Observations of actual reporter-source relationships indicate the second model is the most common. In Gieber and Johnson's study of city hall reporters in a small suburban California community, for example, reporters were found to discuss readily their role as independent checks on the operations of the sources. The reporters regarded sources as poor judges of what is news and preferred to have all the information available to them so they could sift through it themselves and decide on dissemination. The reporters said they had a license to gather all the news and disseminate it as they saw fit.

In actuality, however, the reporters *behaved* somewhat differently. Two of the four reporters working in the community acknowledged that they found themselves writing for the sources rather than their editors or the audience. The two reporters for the local weeklies expressed strong loyalties to the city they were covering. "A weekly reporter is a representative of the city," one said. "It's my city, right or wrong." All four reporters agreed that the sources were justified in withholding the news of a proposed annexation by the city at the time of the study. The sources felt the information might jeopardize the action and wanted it disseminated as a *fait accompli.*

In addition to specific values, the reporters shared with their sources several elemental values concerning government, and these served to bring the two parties even closer together. And despite the fact that the four reporters represented four different newspapers, they communicated with each other regularly, providing each other with support for their decisions regarding dissemination of the news. This interaction reinforced the reporter-source relationships.

The relationships between the reporters and the sources in the California community observed by Gieber and Johnson were not those desired by the sources. The sources sought community consensus. To achieve that end they sought to assimilate the reporters into their frame of reference—make them share the values of the official representatives of the city. The observed relationships were in keeping with the second model of reporter-source relationships in which there is some overlap of goals, but considerable independence as well. In the city studied, the two parties agreed to cooperate for their mutual advantage. The reporters gained access to information and thought they contributed to good government. The sources gained access to the electorate for much the same end.

Studies conducted in other settings have shown much the same pattern. A study of three television beat reporters working for separate outlets in a medium-sized midwestern market, for example, found all three reporters willing to cooperate with their sources to gain access to information. While the study was being conducted and the behavior of the three was being observed, two of three reporters picked up information of wrongdoing by city officials. Neither did anything to follow up on the story.

One of the most noticeable aspects of one of the television reporter's behavior was his reluctance to broach subjects that he thought his sources would not want to discuss. To avoid this, he often went off the record to obtain information: when asked not to use certain information, he obeyed. The reporter's explanation for this behavior was that both he and the city officials were interested in the "welfare of the city." In many ways, the city officials seem to have been successful in co-opting this reporter. At least one of the other reporters, however, remained more independent and better illustrates the second model of Gieber and Johnson.

Studies of reporters in various other settings support the findings that the most common reporter-source relationship involves some sharing of values and goals. The model considered the ideal by the reporter as well as the model desired by most sources isn't very common. These two models, however, do represent end points on a continuum of reporter-source relationships. Some relationships are more like the ideal reportorial situation. Others more closely approximate that desired by the source.

Most of these studies have examined beat reporters, attempting to describe their relationships with sources relied on every day in the usual "walking" of the beat. General assignment reporters, of course, have fewer enduring relationships. Because the duration of the relationship is likely to be short, little common ground can be established. But such reporters nonetheless must bargain with their sources for any given story, and both sides know the bargaining strategy most likely to produce their ends. Even these relationships can be examined in light of the Gieber and Johnson models.

The value of such models is that they provide perspective for examining information gatherers as they go about the task of putting together news stories for mass distribution. When human sources are involved, that gathering often involves a series of compromises designed to aid the gatherers as well as the sources. Reporters are selling access to an information channel and, eventually, an audience. Most sources need that access. Sources, in turn, are selling information or at least easy access to the information. Each party has a commodity highly valued by the other. The final news product sent to the audience member is certainly compromised by the bargaining between reporters and sources.

TECHNOLOGICAL CONSTRAINTS

As we have already seen, reporters, editors, and all media professionals work within certain constraints imposed on them by the technology they employ. In many regards, these forces are external to the communication process. They affect it only because the mass communication process could not exist without technology.

The approximately 1750 daily and 8000 weekly newspapers published in the United States, together with the approximately 7500 radio and television stations, are parts of a vast technological system designed to disseminate information from a large number of sources to a larger number of audience members. This system includes some highly developed information handling facilities, aided and controlled by computers. It also includes some relatively simple components: typewriters, tape recorders, and presses. Every reporter and editor works within the confines of this technology.

The most serious constraint imposed is *time*. Information gatherers and processors for the print and broadcast industry work under tremendous time pressures imposed by the ever-present deadline. For the print media, deadline is determined by the beginning of the press run, which in turn is determined by circulation or distributional factors. In the broadcast media, the deadline is determined by the programming and scheduling that are crucial to the industry. The broadcast media function in terms of the time: they sell time, work to fill time, and define their broadcast day in terms of the time they are on the air.

For the information gatherer, this means that decisions are made with an eye toward the clock. Materials that may be relevant, but are not easily available, may have to be eliminated from at least the first day's account. After the deadline, the reporter may reason, he or she will have time to flesh out the story. Better to get the bare bones story out first.

For the information processor, decisions on which stories to use and which to eliminate are made under the same pressures. But an additional problem arises for this media professional. Seldom is all the information needed to make news decisions available when required. The editor receives a wire service budget, which tells what stories are scheduled to be moved across the wire. But the budget doesn't provide much detail, and the editor must guess a good deal about the story's importance. The wire budget also doesn't include breaking news, though such news is often more important in the long run than the scheduled. Parallel problems develop for local copy. It is often impossible to anticipate what copy will be available until it is too late. Editors must move copy to the composing room as deadline approaches. Inside pages must be filled early. Yet the decisions are made in part without the information needed to make them.

Sociologist Gaye Tuchman, in fact, has argued that though newspeople use terms like *hard* and *soft* to describe the news they handle, such content descriptions are unimportant. The real differences in stories have to do with how they are affected by such things as the time constraints and deadlines imposed by technology. In other words, though newspeople don't often use the terms, stories can be thought of as either *scheduled* or *unscheduled*. Events such as press conferences and meetings are scheduled and easily planned for. Fires, crimes, and natural catastrophes are difficult to handle because they defy planning. They are the stories that make editors long for retirement and reporters hope for promotion to editorships.

For the print media, of course, deadlines have a long history, dating back to the days of heavy street sales and intense market competition. Neither exist much today. It is impossible to argue that the broadcast media play the role the print media played in earlier times. But old habits die slowly, and immediacy is still an important part of the news operation. Because delivery schedules are difficult and expensive to alter, pages expensive to reformat, and work schedules almost impossible to modify, the print media lack flexibility. On that front, at least, the broadcast media have the edge.

That isn't to argue the news personnel of the broadcast media aren't concerned about deadlines. As indicated above, the format of the media makes it essential that news be processed with an eye toward time constraints. But it is easier to interrupt the routines of the broadcast media, at least from a technological perspective, than the routines of the newspapers.

News gatherers and processors in the broadcast media, however, have their own burdens. Stories must be short. Little more than the information often provided in a newspaper headline is used in most radio broadcasts. And while television news departments are generally given more time, it is rarely more than the first few paragraphs of a newspaper story.

Television crews also are expensive, and consequently, small in number at most stations. To maximize return on investment, crews are sent where there is considerable likelihood they will produce usable footage, which usually means action footage. In television news departments, "talking heads"— footage featuring little more than people discussing something—is deadly and to be avoided at almost any cost. As a consequence, assignments are made with an eye toward the visual as well as the nonvisual information in the story. Stories that develop from interviews are passed over in favor of those with considerable visual diversity. In some cases, this means passing over the significant for the trivial. In addition, the high value placed on action film footage intensifies the traditional news tendency to emphasize conflict. Sometimes, the conflict exists more on film than in reality.

ECONOMIC CONSTRAINTS

In both the print and broadcast news media, technology interacts with financial concerns in determining message construction and transmission. In our society the media exist because they can sell advertisements. They can sell these advertisements because they have an audience for the advertisers' products. In other words, advertisers are buying access to an audience.

For newspapers, the problem is more long-term than short. Most readers get their papers from carriers, and the stories in any given issue have relatively little effect on sales. But readers who aren't getting the stories they want from their newspapers may eventually decide they aren't worth the price being paid.

For the broadcast media, however, the effects of the content of a broadcast may be more immediate and of more consequence. There is, by and large, more television competition within the average market than newspaper competition. Viewers can choose from alternative channels. Viewers mean dollars immediately, as the broadcast media must sell time to their advertisers on the basis of the ratings. Since there is evidence viewers have a tendency to leave their channel selectors unchanged for long periods after intially selecting a program, the evening news broadcasts, which precede the lucrative prime-time programming, are of critical importance. News is an important commodity that must be packaged and presented to sell.

The salability of the news product affects the news operation rather directly. The media invest heavily in their news gathering and processing staffs and facilities. When their product doesn't sell, budget cuts sometimes become necessary. These cuts can affect the news product rather dramatically because a small news staff operating on a tight budget often can afford to do little more than process information provided it by sources such as government and industry public relations specialists. Other information is ignored because it lacks a proponent, and the media thus become channels for those hired to send their messages. Tight budgets also affect the quality of the staff that can be assembled and the ability of the newspaper or broadcast outlet to hold those with talent.

Tight budgets also limit the flexibility of the media in their communication activities. It costs money to pre-empt normal programming to provide special coverage of important local and national events. In addition to the expense of producing these specials, the advertising revenue from the prescheduled programs may be lost.

For newspapers, the comparable decision is to increase the news hole of a given edition to accommodate an important event. This can be done by cutting back on other news copy, cutting out scheduled advertising, or increasing the number of pages available. The last two options cost money.

Tight budgets also affect the technology available to the news departments. Improved presses, sophisticated editing facilities, and modern newsroom facilities cost money. And while they are designed to improve the dissemination of messages, they can be implemented only when the news product is returning a profit.

The news business is generally a very profitable one, and it is possible to overestimate the importance of the economic cycle. From the point of view of many press critics, publishers and broadcast license holders ought to show more concern for their audiences and less for the balance sheets. While there may be some merit in such an argument, it is clear the balance sheets are important in the daily operation of the media as they now exist. They affect the flow of information between environmental source and audience member just as certainly as do the other factors discussed here. It is wishful to think otherwise.

THE REPORTER'S TOOLS

Other constraints in the flow of information through the news channels or barriers to communication result directly from the way the reporting task itself is performed. Reporters, or the information gatherers in the mass communication process, learn either from training or experience to use certain techniques to assemble the ingredients of a news story. Imperfections in the techniques lead to messages that imperfectly represent the environment from which they were drawn.

The reporter has essentially two ways of knowing what is going on in the environment. He or she can observe firsthand that segment of interest in the environment. Or the reporter can learn about the environment from someone else who had firsthand contact. The reporter who witnesses a fire and writes a story about it is employing the *direct* observational method. The reporter who hears about the fire from the police or firemen and writes a story based on these accounts is using *indirect* observation. In the second situation, the report is based entirely on what sources have told the reporter about the event.

It is difficult to say precisely what proportion of the information that appears in the newspaper or is broadcast is generated from direct observation and what proportion comes from indirect observation. Studies of selected newspapers, however, have indicated that upwards of three-quarters of the stories result primarily from information provided by sources.

One of the difficulties of such analyses, of course, is that many stories employ both observational techniques. Few reporters ever witness a fire from beginning to end, and those who do probably find themselves the target of grand jury arson investigations. Instead, reporters combine the information they obtain from their own observations with those of the police and firemen, those whose property was damaged by the fire, neighbors, and any others who witnessed something relevant. The final story is a meshing of information from several independent observations.

The problem with information obtained from nonmedia observers is that it may be misinformation. To continue with the fire report example, the police and firemen weren't present when the fire started, unless again, they had some suspicious connection with its beginning. So what they tell the reporter may have been surmised or learned from others. As the length of the information chain increases, the chance of distortion increases. The police and firemen may unwittingly provide incorrect information or leave out important circumstances or details when they give their accounts. The neighbors may overemphasize unimportant details or may selectively recall only certain details. The result is that the reporter's account of the occurrence may have little similarity to the actual occurrence.

The reporter's observations can have many of these same flaws as well. Since most reporters are human (Clark Kent being a notable and fictitious exception), they can fail to observe relevant aspects of any given event. They can fail to take accurate notes on what they did observe, forget to use what they did take notes about, or simply make incorrect use of the information gathered.

If none of these observational flaws were present, two trained reporters sent to cover the same story from the same vantage point would produce exactly the same mental and physical notes on the story. The two might not write exactly the same story, or use the same information, because of differences in news judgment. But the observations would be the same.

Reporters with more than one fire's experience, however, will be quick to note how unlikely it is that such a compatible pair of observations would be produced. Fires are relatively simple things, as story materials go, so the likelihood of two reporters producing identical written or mental notes on more complex matters is even smaller. When the story involves both direct observation and information obtained indirectly from sources, the possibility of identical pairs of notes being produced is probably almost zero.

This whole process of selection is shown in a simplified form in figure 7.2. On the left-hand side of the figure, we have a series of elements of any given event, labeled here as E_1 to E_{10}. In a fire story, these elements might be the size of the flames, the number of firemen present, the size of the crowd gathering to watch. The two reporters on the scene, perhaps because of differences in where they were standing or differences in focus, select—often unconsciously—specific elements for their observations. Reporter XX selected five of these elements. Report YY selected six. There is overlap on three. Now XX and YY rush back to their offices and write their stories. But they are working from slightly different sets of observations. The stories produced do

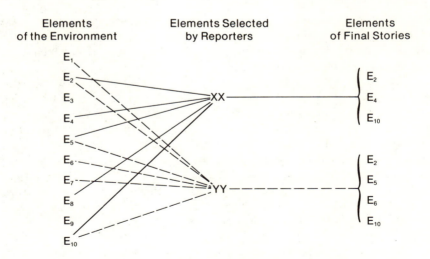

Fig. 7.2 Two Reporters Observing an Environment

not include the same elements. Each writer has reduced the number of elements again and in doing so modified the event somewhat. By necessity, the two accounts must differ since the observations, though of the same event, were different.

Historically, reporters have had rather few guidelines for obtaining information either by direct or indirect observation. The result has been, in part, that reporters have come to rely rather heavily on *expert sources*—those who are supposed to know. So when a reporter is given an assignment to learn about the nature of fires in his or her community, their cycles, if any, and the areas most commonly hit, the reporter is likely to turn to some expert, such as the fire marshall. When a reporter is told to learn about public sentiment prior to a crucial election between two factions of city government, the reporter often turns to the political "pros."

In both examples, the reporter probably made a mistake. In the fire story example, the reporter would be better advised to go to the fire records and analyze them. The fire marshall probably hasn't done that, but that's what is needed to get the story accurately. In the second example, the reporter probably should have located someone who had good survey or poll data assessing public opinion. Or the reporter could have conducted such a survey on his or her own. Most old pros (though clearly fewer of the new ones) rely on samplings of opinion that can often be in error.

A recent trend in journalism has been reporters doing just the kinds of things we've recommended for our fictitious reporters. The trend is nicknamed *precision journalism,* and it is based on the premise that reporters today need better *observational tools* than those used in the past.

Many reporters are turning to the tools of the social scientists, such as the sample survey and the field experiment, in an effort to improve their observations of the local community. Essentially, these journalists are seeking reporting techniques that allow them to eliminate or at least reduce the biases in their own, direct observations. They also are seeking ways of decreasing the reliance on sources when they are not needed so as to eliminate this potential contaminant in the information gathering process. Finally, these reporters are trying to find ways of reducing the error introduced by reliance on sources when no alternative exists.

The decision of these journalists to turn to the social scientist is quite appropriate. Both groups share a desire to observe the social environment so that it can be described *precisely,* without distortion. Social scientists generally call this a concern with *validity.* They want to be as sure as possible that the observational tools, or measures, they use represent social reality. Social scientists recognize this is a difficult task, but it is a central concern of their disciplines.

A related concern has to do with *reliability,* or stability. In other words, techniques of observation are considered to be better if they can be used by different observers at the same time, or by the same observer at different times, and yet get the same result. Reporters who observe different things about the same fire haven't employed reliable measures. Since unreliable measures can't adequately represent the environmental phenomenon under study, they aren't valid either.

Perhaps the most popular observational tool borrowed by journalists from the social scientists has been the scientific survey. The survey, or poll, which can help reporters accurately assess public opinion, has become a standard part of election reporting. In the 1976 presidential primaries, for example, survey teams from both NBC and CBS, the latter working with the *New York Times,* were in the field interviewing scientifically selected voters as they left the polls. Their goal was not only to predict the election results before the official tallies were in, but also, and more importantly, to learn *why* people were voting as they were. The stories produced from the poll data were a crucial part of the *Times* primary election coverage. Similar polls were conducted in the fall general election as well. *Times* reporters, and others at newpapers and broadcast outlets around the country, were using the scientific survey to better tell the story of the elections.

In fact, pollsters and newspapers have had a long history of joint endeavors. The Gallup and Harris polls are supported by the news media that purchase the stories they generate. Reporters, in fact, have been involved in election prediction almost since the beginning of U.S. elections.

What is different about this new use of surveys is the extent to which the newspapers and networks are generating their own data and the uses to which these data are being put. The polls are no longer seen only as means of *predicting* results a few hours or days before the polls close. They also are a means of *explaining* the results to the readers. → *P l u S ? ?*

Polls also are being recognized as mechanisms of assessing public opinion on a wide range of topics not connected with electoral politics. With polling techniques, too, reporters can reduce reliance on secondary sources and go directly to the origins of the information—in this case, the people themselves.

Reporters also have begun to reexamine the masses of data gathered by the government, often under the direction of trained social scientists, as potential bases for previously untouched stories. Census Bureau data, for example, can be used to plot changes in local communities and to suggest policy needed to forestall crises. Local records on property tax assessment, marriage license purchases, medical treatment, and school expenditures can be used in similar ways. The reporter, aided by the computer, can reduce these massive files to meaningful information that previously was unavailable.

Less progress has been made in improving the standard, direct observational methods of the reporter, but awareness of the problems has probably increased. Social scientists term this kind of information gathering *participant observation*—though the degree of participation often varies. Social scientists employing this method have gained an increased awareness of their own biases and how the observers influence those being studied. Reporters too seem to be gaining this social sensitivity to the problems of gathering such information.

The outcome of this trend toward use of social science techniques in the field of journalism should be improved message production. These new tools allow for a reduction of distortion in the information-gathering stage of the mass communication process. To the extent they succeed, the chances increase that the messages actually transmitted to the audience member closely resemble the environment in which they were generated. These precision tools help break down some of the many barriers to communication.

CONCLUSION

In this and the preceding chapter we have examined factors that affect professional communicators as they gather information and prepare it for dissemination to the audience. Previous chapters examined audience members' role in determining the success or failure of communication. If successful mass communication is indexed by the understanding audience members have of their environment, then the behavior of the professional communicator must be scrutinized as well.

The crucial process in news production and dissemination is *selection*. The reporter selects from all the stimuli present in the environment only certain ones for inclusion in the message he or she produces. Local editors select from the reporters' copy those stories and facts to be transmitted to the audience and determine the kind of display they will be given. A similar set of decisions is made by the wire editor who selects from all the copy presented him or her from the wire services. These editors operate under the direction of the news managers who oversee the whole production operation and determine the overall makeup of the news products. Only after these decisions have been made is the message put into a form that can be distributed to the audience members.

The decisions these various professionals make—each of them a gatekeeper—are influenced by a series of factors. The *attitudes* of the reporters and editors toward the topic appear to have some influence, as do their *social backgrounds* and *previous experiences*. Newspeople approach their jobs holding certain predispositions to behave and react in certain ways to what they learn in their official capacities.

But reporters and editors also bring a set of *professional values* to the situation that, to some extent, offset their personal reactions and prescribe behaviors appropriate for the task. These values are taught in colleges and universities and form part of a general system of beliefs about press performance in this country. While there is not perfect agreement regarding these values, there is evidence of *some* sharing of outlook. There is little to suggest that in the abstract many professionals disagree on the essential characteristics of news.

The *policy* of the news operation may or may not support these individual values. News personnel are likely to go along with the newspaper or broadcast station policy regardless of apparent conflict, partly because of the *social support* professionals obtain from their colleagues. It appears that if one is going to sin, it is better to have fellow sinners as colleagues. Another reason the policy of the owners or managers can be obeyed without great difficulty is that the values are, in many ways, vague statements with little concrete link to actual decision making. It often is difficult to determine when a clear violation has taken place.

Most news decisions are made with the audience in mind—at least if the journalist's professional values are given credence. Since the audience is amorphous in many respects, most decisions can be defended by such a reference. The journalist also has the option of claiming that only he or she has the right to determine what the audience needs, even if the audience has expressed dissatisfaction in the past. So while there seems to be agreement regarding definition of news, there often is considerable disagreement regarding specific news judgments.

The journalist also is restricted in his or her work by the nature of the *relationships developed with sources*. Since much of what the journalist gathers for dissemination is obtained from other persons, the relationship between the reporter and the source is a prime factor in determining what the audience member receives. It appears that most reporters compromise their values slightly in dealing with sources. And sources do likewise. The result is a product more to the liking of both parties than would otherwise be obtained.

Finally, the journalist is restricted by the *technology* of the mass communication system and the *tools* available for the gathering of information. Technology both shapes the format of messages and determines content. Available techniques for gathering information restrict the news channel at its origin.

Some who read these descriptions of the behaviors of working journalists may use them as an excuse for flaws in their own behavior once they actually are on the job. It is easy to understand why that would happen. In fact, part of the defense journalists develop by colleagual interplay to justify their small sins is based on the view that they are restricted by a myriad of forces. To some extent, that is a reasonable defense.

Our intent here is to describe these factors so the reader is aware of them and can learn to deal with them. We subscribe to the ideals of most working journalists and are interested in ways of seeing them implemented. That can happen only when journalists understand the constraints. In the same way that it is necessary to understand the barriers that audience members erect to produce successful communication, it also is necessary to understand the barriers erected by the journalists, their colleagues, and their work setting. Then we may have communication.

PART THREE
THE
COMMUNITY

8
The Communication Institution and Society

On Sunday, June 13, 1971, the *New York Times* carried a two-deck headline across four columns at the top of page one. The headline read: "Vietnam Archive: Pentagon Study Traces 3 Decades of Growing U.S. Involvement."

For the *Times,* that first story by reporter Neil Sheehan was the culmination of nearly three months of research by a team of reporters and editors. But it was also the beginning—though the *Times* reporters only sensed it at the time—of one of the most dramatic conflicts between the press and government in U.S. history.

The June 13 articles were intended to be the first in a ten-part series of lengthy reports on what has come to be known as the Pentagon Papers. On June 16, the *Times* series was stopped because the U.S. government had successfully obtained a court order halting publication. For the first time in U.S. history, a newspaper had been restrained *in advance* from printing a specific news story.

Before the legal battle was over, and the Supreme Court had ruled six to three in favor of the press's right to print without prior restraint, the government had moved against three papers in addition to the *Times*—the *Washington Post,* the *Boston Globe,* and the *St. Louis Post-Dispatch.*

For members of the press and government as well as the public at large, the Pentagon Papers episode was indeed dramatic. Sanford Ungar, a reporter for the *Washington Post* during the period who later chronicled the events in a book titled *The Papers & The Papers,* has quoted former Defense Secretary Clark Clifford as saying that the Pentagon Papers episode "was an event of outstanding significance. . . . I had never seen anything like it in 26 years."

For the social scientist, the events surrounding publication of the Pentagon Papers were perhaps equally dramatic, though somewhat predictable. The conflict was, after all, a rather open exchange between two major institutions of society. The executive branch of government was defending what it thought to be its right to keep certain documents secret. The press was asserting what it considered to be its right to print whatever information it obtained. The Supreme Court, arbitrator for the conflict, gave its nod to the press in this battle. In other battles over differing issues, the press has lost. Government cannot use prior restraint to prohibit libel, for example. But it can legislate penalties for published acts that unjustly injure a person's reputation.

The news media are institutions within a society. As such, they are influenced by—and they influence—other institutions. There is a certain amount of give and take in our social system. The press is nudged one way by government, another by the business establishment. But the press does plenty of nudging of its own. The nudging—or pushing and shoving—of institutions within a society has great impact, albeit indirect, on the messages reporters send and audience members receive.

THE HISTORICAL CONTEXT

Since Johann Gutenberg printed his first book using movable type—an event that signaled the beginnings of modern mass communications—there have been two *major* concepts of what the relationships between the press and the larger society should be. The older concept has been labeled the *authoritarian* approach to communications by Fred Siebert, Theodore Peterson, and Wilbur Schramm, who have written extensively about concepts of press and society relationships. The other concept, called the *libertarian* approach, underlies many of the formalized rules of press behavior in the United States. The First Amendment to the U.S. Constitution, which was used by the Supreme Court in deciding the Pentagon Papers case, is a clear statement of libertarian principles.

Out of each of these two major concepts of press-society relationships a modern variant has grown. The *communistic* view of the press is a variant of the authoritarian concept. A *social responsibility* stance is an outgrowth of the libertarian concept.

The role assigned the press by a society is always a reflection of the basic assumptions that underlie the society itself. The philosophical assumptions about the natures of man and of society, the role of the state and the individual's relationship to the state, and the mechanisms for discovering, and the nature of truth all influence the role assigned the press.

Gutenberg printed his book in an authoritarian society. The state was considered to rank higher than the individual, and only through serving the state could the individual obtain fulfillment. In such a society, the state was given a certain amount of power as caretaker or overseer of the individual, who was considered dependent on the state.

For the most part, truth was considered the province of the elite of society. All persons were not thought to possess it equally—or even be capable of understanding it. Rather, the ruling class was entrusted with the knowledge existing in the social system.

The technological developments after Gutenberg gave the press the potential for threatening such a social order by making information available to all, regardless of class. The ruling elite then began to control access to printing facilities in order to control content. That made it unnecessary to restrict use of the printed materials by the masses.

In such a way—by issuing licenses to printers, threatening punishment after publication for treason or sedition, paying or bribing writers—the rulers were eventually able to adapt the modern press to the old social order. The press became another tool for promoting social consensus and maintaining the old social order. The ethic governing use of the media was clear: all publishing should contribute to the maintenance and health of society. By aiding society, the press would be serving the common man, since the state was the commoner's keeper.

While the authoritarian concept of press behavior is no longer the only concept in existence, it still holds in many societies. The modern version, adopted in many communistic countries, makes many of the same assumptions about the role of the press.

In many of these communistic societies, the communication institutions are conceived of as instruments of government. They are assigned roles by the state, and perform for the state. There is little or no private ownership of the media.

Unlike the media in the authoritarian societies, the press is not merely restricted in what it does. It is integrated into the social system and assigned a role. The activities of the media are planned—programmed—to serve the state. In a sense, the modern communistic concept is simply a better worked out authoritarian scheme for making the press serve the established order.

The sixteenth and seventeenth centuries were periods of great change in Western Europe. Developments in the sciences seemed to vindicate the power of human reason. The Reformation challenged the authority of the Catholic church, and the growth of a middle class challenged the existing social stratification. It was also a period of political upheaval.

The libertarian concept of mass communications developed in this period and was nurtured in the intellectual climate of the Enlightenment. During this time, a belief in the capability of the individual to comprehend the complexities of the world without recourse to supernatural evaluation was given support.

Intellectuals of the time declared their independence from the outside restrictions of the authoritarian social system. The old bonds were beginning to become undone.

While the authoritarian principles held that man was dependent on the state, the philosophers who laid the groundwork for the libertarian concept of the press thought man to be independent and rational. He was thought capable of choosing between truth and falsity. While the authoritarians believed the state outranked the individual, the libertarians argued that the state existed only to provide the proper setting for man to develop his potentialities. The state existed at the will of the people. It should be cast aside if it did not fulfill its function of offering the proper framework for the betterment of the individual.

The task of society in the libertarian view was to provide a free marketplace of ideas so that people can exercise the gift of reason. From the exchange of the marketplace, truth is expected to emerge. Government is not to interfere with the exchange of information, for in doing so it could easily prohibit the surfacing of truth. No viewpoint or opinion should be silenced because of the risk of silencing the expression of truth.

In the libertarian view, the *press* was a part of the marketplace. It provided the forum through which ideas could be exchanged and truth given its opportunity to emerge. The media were to be privately owned. Competition in an open market would result in the silencing of useless press outlets as customers refused to provide support. The voices of reason would prevail.

The U.S. Constitution was written by libertarians. The press system established for the country was designed with libertarian goals in mind. The First Amendment to the Constitution remains even today one of the clearest statements of the libertarian principle of press freedom:

> Congress shall make no law respecting an establishment of religion or prohibiting the free exercise thereof; or *abridging the freedom of speech, or of the press;* or the right of the people peaceably to assemble, and to petition the Government for a redress of grievances.

This statement of press freedom was surrounded by basic libertarian statements regarding freedom of religion and speech, the right to assembly, and the right to ask government to respond to the needs of the people. The statement was absolute.

It failed, however, to anticipate much of what followed in the development of mass communications in the United States. After the middle of the nineteenth century, the media began to become more commercial than they had been at the time the Constitution was written. They relied more on advertising revenue than political support or circulation income. And it became very expensive to purchase the equipment necessary to gain access to the free marketplace of ideas. As a result, unpopular ideas did not get exposure in the marketplace.

Libertarians also did not anticipate the birth of broadcasting. Theoretically, at least, everyone can purchase a printing press and begin a newspaper. But everyone cannot have access to the very limited number of broadcast channels. Someone had to prevent chaos and protect the public's interest. So the government stepped in, despite the absolute wording of the First Amendment.

The growth in the size of the individual press institutions and the resulting inability of newcomers to enter the market, the frequent suppression of minority views not popular enough to survive the marketplace, and the advent of broadcasting all signaled the end to a strictly libertarian approach to the press in the United States. Rather than extending the press's freedom, government and civic leaders began to examine the media's performance. They began to argue that with freedom go certain responsibilities to the society of which the press is a part.

Under this social responsibility concept of the press, society can expect from its media system "intelligent accounts of the day's events in a context which gives them meaning," to quote from the report of the Hutchins commission on freedom of the press. The commission, chaired by Robert Maynard Hutchins, president of the University of Chicago, issued a report in 1947 that stands today as one of the clearest statements of this concept of press responsibilities.

The commission assigned government a much different role in dealing with the press than libertarians had envisioned. If the media do not provide needed services to the individual members of society, the government must step in, the Hutchins commission said. The press is not an adjunct of government, under this concept. It still serves the role of watchdog and critic. But the government is given some encouragement to act to improve the performance of the media. For instance, the social responsibility concept provides a rationale for the government regulation of the broadcast industry.

For those espousing the social responsibility viewpoint, the media serve an important function. They provide for a smoother functioning of society. The media are to continue to provide discourse on the day's events. But it is to be done responsibly. The end product, according to proponents, should be an elevation of the discussion in the marketplace "from the plane of violence to the plane of discussion," in the words of the Hutchins commission.

The press system in the United States does not operate wholly under either the libertarian or the social responsibility theories. In a sense, the social responsibility concept is simply a revision of the older principle. So far, the media in the United States have been able to function without bringing the two concepts into complete unison.

MASS COMMUNICATION

Sociologists use the term *mass communication* to differentiate mass from other, particularly interpersonal, communication. The printing of the Pentagon Papers by the *New York Times* was an attempt at mass communication. The discussions among the editors and lawyers for the *Times* led to the mass communication, but in and of themselves these discussions were quite different. They were interpersonal, rather than mass, in nature.

British sociologist Denis McQuail has listed several distinguishing characteristics of mass communication that bear repeating. First, mass communication, as compared with interpersonal communication, involves different kinds of participants. The actors in the mass process are collectivities rather than individuals. Mass communication is complex, involving organized groups of message producers and large audiences. The message is transmitted through a complex system and intended for a largely undifferentiated audience. In other words, a highly organized sender produces and transmits messages to a largely unorganized audience. This is quite different from the simple setting of interpersonal communications where one person interacts communicatively with another.

The second characteristic listed by McQuail has to do with the technology used in the mass communication process: it facilitates one-way communication. Direct feedback from the audience members to the sender is relatively difficult. The technology also allows the sender and receiver of the message to be great distances apart. Unlike the interpersonal setting, which requires proximity for communication (telephone assisted communications being one exception), the mass communication activity can take place when the sender and receiver are greatly distant.

The technology also adds another difference between mass and interpersonal communications. Because the technology is expensive, access is difficult. While everyone can engage in interpersonal communication, few have the opportunity to communicate to the masses.

The relationship between the sender and receiver in mass communication is quite distinct from the relationship in interpersonal settings. In the former, the relationship is not interactive in any real sense. The participants are distanced from each other physically, linked only by the technology, designed for one-way communication. The result is that the communication between sender and receiver lacks the exchange present in interpersonal communication, where direct feedback is possible and there is proximity.

The content of mass communication, finally, is quite different from the usual content of interpersonal communication. Mass communication messages are largely undifferentiated, aimed at many members of the social system. Interpersonal messages, on the other hand, are individualized. They are intended to play on the similarities of the parties to the communication. Mass messages cannot have such a focus. They are intended for large numbers of people and therefore include little individualized content.

The characteristics of mass communication make mass communication more difficult than interpersonal communication. Mass communication is unbalanced or asymmetrical. The parties are different. The technology is cumbersome. Interaction is limited, and the content impersonal. It is somewhat surprising communication takes place at all!

FUNCTIONS
OF MASS COMMUNICATION

But mass communication does take place. The media do serve the societies in which they operate, and they serve definite social functions.

These functions are not, however, always the ones intended by the leaders of the society. As we have seen in the discussion of the historical developments underlying modern press systems, societies attempt to use the media in different ways to achieve these functions. But there seems to be little doubt the media serve some of the same *functions* in all societies.

One of the pioneers of research in mass communication, political scientist Harold Lasswell, noted three major *activities* of mass media. First, the media *survey* the societal environment, that is, they collect and distribute information regarding what is going on in the environment. The media present what is usually labeled the news of the day. Second, the media *interpret* the environment and prescribe, largely through editorial page activity, proper reactions to the environment. Finally, the media *transmit the social heritage* from generation to generation by communicating values and social norms to members of the society, particularly those entering anew or from another social system.

Sociologist Charles Wright, who has elaborated on the Lasswell paradigm considerably, has added a fourth type of communication behavior. The media quite simply provide communication content intended for amusement, irrespective of other consequences they may produce. The media *entertain*.

These are the activities of the mass communication institutions. But what are the consequences for society? What societal functions do the activities serve? Are the consequences always those intended by the communicator?

Clearly there is a difference between the purpose behind the communication and the consequence. The writer of a series of stories on a local health problem, for example, may intend merely to inform audience members, but the consequence might be panic on the part of audience members.

It also is worth distinguishing between positive and negative functions. Consequences that are undesirable from the point of view of the society are often labeled *dysfunctions*. A communicative activity can produce both positive functions and negative dysfunctions.

According to sociologist Wright, the *surveillance* activities of the media serve several important societal functions. First, these activities—the news-gathering and disseminating behaviors of the media—warn the population of impending threats and dangers, such as those resulting from natural disasters or international, military conflicts. Warnings in the mass media may have the additional function of promoting egalitarianism or feelings of equality. Every member of the society seems to have an equal chance of protecting himself or herself from dangers.

The surveillance activity also is crucial for routine functioning of institutions within the society. The business community, for example, depends on the media to some extent for stock market information. Farmers depend on the media for weather information as well as information about the worth of their products. The transportation industry depends on the media for information on local traffic conditions.

The media also serve what Wright has termed an ethicizing function. They define for individuals within society what is normal or accepted behavior, and consequently, they help to strengthen society's control on its members. This ethicizing usually results from routine activities, such as reporting of crimes or other types of "deviant" behavior. By making known to the individual society members what is punished, or out of the usual, the media reinforce the definition of "normal" behavior. As a consequence, few members of the society are unaware of the inappropriateness of certain behaviors.

The surveillance activity of the media can be dysfunctional as well as functional, Wright has noted. For example, while the news in the media serve a warning function, they also can lead to responses such as panic. Hysterical responses, of course, are not in the best interest of the society. The media also can ill serve a society by presenting to members information about other social systems. Such information often leads to discontent. In other words, the media can help create a sense of dissatisfaction within a society by showing audience members what other societies have achieved. In some cases, this results in social unrest that actually prevents the society's leaders from achieving more modest goals.

Perhaps the most important function for society of the news media's *interpretive* activities is to prevent undesirable consequences. On occasion, the creation of false expectations, or even panic, can result from the news dissemination and surveillance activity. By commenting on the news, the media can focus attention on selected developments and prescribe appropriate responses. But this activity also can be dysfunctional. The same media behavior that serves to restrict social turmoil also may impede needed social change. The society failing to change in an ever more complex system of interconnected societies will probably experience severe difficulties.

By *transmitting the culture* from the elders of society to its newer members the media serve an important socialization function. They increase understanding of the society, thereby laying the groundwork for social cohesion. They widen the base of common norms and experiences. This same activity can be dysfunctional, for it can foster alienation within the system. Since the media are relatively impersonal communicators, societies may be ill-advised in assigning too large a *socialization* role to the media. More personal means of transmission of culture, such as those provided by the schools, may be more suitable.

The *entertainment* activity of the media may be both functional and dysfunctional as well. Certainly such media content is helpful in providing respite to troubled members of the society. But it also may provide too much diversion from serious consideration of societal problems. It is difficult to know what level of entertainment is most appropriate for any given social unit.

These are, then, some of the functions the media can serve for a society. These functions result from normal media behavior and are the consequences of what the media do as part of the mass communication act.

What are the forces within the social setting that determine the media activities—which either are functional or dysfunctional for the social order? What do the other institutions of society do to influence press behavior?

LEGAL BARRIERS
TO MASS COMMUNICATION

Every social system erects legal barriers to mass communication. The barriers are the result of basic assumptions in that society about the social milieu, and as we have seen, can be classified into two major types as suggested by Siebert, Peterson, and Schramm. The first major type of barrier is authoritarian; a modern version is the communistic theory. The second major type is libertarian, from which the social responsibility concept developed.

In the United States, of course, the press is well protected by the First Amendment to the Constitution. Congress is not allowed to restrict or limit freedom of speech or of the press. Passage of the Fourteenth Amendment to the Constitution during the Civil War era extended that principle to the states. In a very general sense, then, the most important legal constraint in this country is against other institutions that might want to control the press.

But that view is a bit too simplistic! The writers of the Constitution did not intend to allow all communications, and they particularly didn't care to protect those involving defamation. To defame a person is to hold that person up to hatred, contempt, or ridicule, or to cause him or her to be shunned or avoided. To do that in print is libel. In speech, it is slander. It has been the interpretation of the courts that the Constitution protects neither. The courts also have ruled that the Constitution does not allow the press to invade the privacy of individuals.

Much communication has not been considered by the courts to be speech at all. Obscene materials, for the most part, have not enjoyed the protection afforded other, socially more accepted forms of communication. In the past, neither the theater nor the movies were afforded the same protection given other forms of speech.

Copyright statutes also are a barrier to communications. They determine when certain kinds of communicated messages become the property of some individual, and they restrict the use of these materials by others. The courts have held that these restrictions are not contrary to the Constitution.

The First Amendment's blanket statement of press freedom also has run into problems of late as reporters and jurists attempt to find ways to insure each individual's right to a fair trial, guaranteed by the Sixth Amendment. Jurors who have read about their case in the newspapers and formed impressions of the defendant's guilt or innocence cannot give an unbiased hearing. The evidence before the court, not that printed in the newspapers or broadcast over the airwaves, is supposed to determine the case. Whatever the solution to the fair trial/free press controversy, the absolute statement of the First Amendment must be altered somewhat. The Sixth Amendment's guarantee places restrictions on what the press can do.

Government agencies also have entered into the business of restricting free expression. The Federal Communications Commission, as noted, restricts the use of the airwaves lest they be hopelessly clogged by those desiring to use them. Federal agencies controlling commerce have restricted advertisers, some of whom have argued that the First Amendment protects all communications, including those that are clearly false and designed to produce commercial gain.

These legal constraints on the press show that complete freedom of the press does not exist in the United States. Perhaps no society can survive such an absolute freedom. Indeed, the pressures on society to increase the restrictions on the press are rather great. To a large degree, the pressures result from changes in the press system since the Constitution was framed 200 years ago. It has become increasingly difficult for most individuals in society to practice freedom of the press, because most people cannot afford to acquire the technological means of mass communication. Press critic A. J. Liebling was pretty much on target when he said that freedom of the press is the inalienable right of any person rich enough to own one.

ECONOMIC CONSTRAINTS ON THE PRESS

Beyond the obvious capital requirements for entry into the world of mass communication, there is an even greater, more binding economic constraint on mass communication in the marketplace. In the United States and Canada, daily newspapers and most broadcasting stations operate as private businesses. If they do not earn enough to cover their expenses, they will disappear from the marketplace. Only a tiny minority of the news outlets in North America are exempt from this requirement.

Because they must earn their own way, the mass media are subject to the economic pressures and constraints of the marketplace. One of the major constraints is the empirical fact that over the years the total number of dollars spent by audiences and advertisers in support of all the mass media taken as a group has been a *constant proportion of the total spending in the marketplace*. In other words, the general state of the economy has determined how much was available to support the mass communication industries.

Audiences and advertisers pay out the dollars that support mass communication. Books and films are totally dependent on audience spending. Broadcasting is dependent on advertisers for its revenues. Newspapers and magazines fall in between, depending on both audience and advertiser spending.

General economic conditions determine the ebb and flow of mass communication, not the degree of competition within the media themselves. Introduction of new mass media—television in the 1940s and 1950s for example— did not increase the amount of money available in the mass communication marketplace. New forms of mass media or changing patterns of competition among existing media only change the way the economic pie is divided up. The size of the pie is determined by the general economy.

This major economic constraint in mass communication is illustrated by the trends in total spending for mass communication over recent decades. In table 8.1 total spending on mass communication—audience expenditures *and* advertiser expenditures—is measured four different ways. For each of the four measures in table 8.1, a steady increase from year to year would yield a score of +1. On the other hand, if the amount of spending each year was consistently less than for the previous year, the total score would be −1. If the trend were constant across time the trend score would be 0. The range of possible score,

Table 8.1 Trends in Total Spending in Mass Media, 1929–68*

In Actual Dollars	+.95
In Constant Dollars (Also Controlling for Population and Personal Income)	+.46
As Percentage of GNP	−.33
As Percentage of Average Personal Income per Household	−.25

* Adapted from Maxwell E. McCombs, "Mass Media in the Marketplace," *Journalism Monographs*, 24 (1972), 8. Reprinted by permission.

then, is −1 to +1, with the sign indicating the direction, and the value indicating the strength of the trend.

First, in terms of the *total number of dollars* spent by consumers and advertisers, there has been a steady increase over recent decades. From $6 billion in 1929, the number of dollars spent on mass media reached nearly $35 billion some forty years later. And that increase has continued over recent years. This trend is reflected by a score of +.95 in table 8.1.

But during this same span of years there were more consumers to spend money as the population grew, average personal income quadrupled, and inflation raised the price of almost everything. So when the trend in total number of dollars spent is corrected for these factors, we find a more realistic score of +.46 for total spending on mass communication.

Other evidence, however, indicates a decline in spending on mass communication over recent decades. Taken as a proportion of Gross National Product (GNP)—the value of all goods and services produced during a year—spending on mass communication shows a moderately declining (−.33) trend. In recent years mass communication expenditures seemed to have settled on a plateau of about 4.25 percent of the GNP.

Another way of looking at the total money spent each year for mass communication is to regard it as a proportion of the average personal income of U.S. households. For nearly a half century these expenditures per household by consumers *and* advertisers have equaled about 5 percent of the average personal income per household in the U.S. But here too the overall trend across time shows a moderate decline (−.25).

While the exact picture of spending patterns on mass communication varies somewhat from measure to measure, the overall picture is that expenditures on mass communication are constrained by the general economic conditions in our society.

INFLUENCE
OF JOURNALISTIC COMPETITION

The economic marketplace creates competition for the news organization. It is, in part, competition for financial resources—usually in the form of advertising revenues and circulation. But competition for the news itself—the raw materials of mass communications—may also influence media behavior.

Many media critics, alarmed at the increasing number of U.S. cities served by newspapers owned by one company, have argued that the result of such noncompetitive situations is a journalistically inferior product. The newspapers in these communities, the argument goes, do not have to perform well because audience members have no alternative. If people in communities served by noncompetitive newspapers want a newspaper that carries any local information, they have to read the noncompetitive product. For persons living

Table 8.2 Number of Local News Stories in Media of Three Ohio Communities during Study Period*

Community 1: Served by Noncompetitive Media	250
Community 2: Served by Competitive Media	290
Community 3: Served by Competitive Media	388

* Adapted from Guido H. Stempel III, "Effects on Performance of a Cross-Media Monopoly," *Journalism Monographs*, 29 (1973), 23. Reprinted by permission.

in almost 98 percent of the approximately 1500 U.S. cities served by a daily newspaper, this is the situation. Only slightly over 2 percent of our cities have a truly competitive newspaper market.

The evidence to support the critic's position, however, is not very convincing. In fact, studies seem to show that *newspaper* competition has very little positive influence on the news product. And there is some evidence such competition can lead to sensationalism and less serious treatment of local news materials.

But the critics may still have a point. There is some evidence that if the news monopoly is complete—if the newspapers don't have any competition for the raw materials of news from even the broadcast news outlets—the journalistic product suffers. The evidence for this conclusion comes from a study of three East Central Ohio communities, all of which were served by only one newspaper, one radio station, and one television station. In one community all three were owned by the same company. In the other two, some form of competition among these media voices existed.

While the findings from the study may not be generalizable to all monopoly situations, they are quite clear in demonstrating what news monopoly meant for the persons living in the total monopoly community. Persons living in that town used the media less and were less informed than residents of the other two communities.

And it is no wonder! The news content of the monopoly media was less comprehensive and less sound journalistically than the content of the media in the other communities. In fact, as table 8.2 illustrates, there was less local news in the monopoly community than in either of the other two locales studied. The news organization in the noncompetitive community did not seem as adept at carrying out the news gathering and disseminating function.

COMMUNITY CONSTRAINTS ON THE PRESS

In addition to the legal and economic constraints imposed on the press by the social system, as well as those imposed by competition from other news operations, constraints are imposed to some degree by the community the press institution serves. In other words, the audience, acting through direct sanction and indirectly through threats of sanction, may influence how the press performs.

The evidence, however, is that editors overstate the case. Editors frequently say, for example, that they would like to do more investigative pieces or write or air more strident editorials, but the community won't tolerate it. In other words, the editor is arguing that the community sets the limits within which the newspaper or broadcast outlet operates.

To some extent, of course, this is true. The media have on occasion been the targets of boycotts by members of a community. And, to be sure, some readers do cancel their papers when they read news stories they find offensive—despite the truth that may underlie them. Viewers and listeners do turn away from broadcast outlets. When the medium is the only one in town, however, people who want media messages can't go elsewhere. And overall the evidence is that audience members appreciate a sound journalistic product.

A study of New England newspapers supports this interpretation. In general, few community characteristics were found to be related to performance of the newspapers operating in them. Good newspapers were published as often in small communities as large ones, in growing as well as declining or stagnant ones, in wealthy communities as well as not-so-wealthy ones. The only community characteristics found to make much difference were the educational level of the community members and their diversity of background. In other words, those communities with better educated residents did have slightly better newspapers in general than those communities with less educated members. And those communities with diverse religious—and, it would seem, ethnic—backgrounds had the better newspapers. But there were many exceptions to the two relationships.

What is even more important, there was a significant relationship between how well the newspaper performed journalistically and how well it circulated in the community served. People were more likely to read the papers in those communities served by newspapers judged to be journalistically sound than in those where the newspaper product was considered deficient. To the readers, it seems, the kind of product made a difference.

ORGANIZATIONAL FACTORS

This same study of New England newspapers tends to show that decisions made within the newsroom and executive offices of newspapers are more important than community characteristics in determining press performance. Size of staff, as well as educational level of the staff, are among those factors strongly related to how well the newspaper serves its communities. The salary paid the staff also is important. To have a good news product the publisher must work at it. Some of the best ways to start are by hiring an appropriately sized staff of well-trained professionals and by rewarding them for the work they do.

Other managerial decisions are important too. The best newspapers attempt to ascertain the wants and needs of the community members. Those papers become involved in various professional organizations aimed at improving the news product. And the papers investing in sound *business* practices tend to produce sound news products. In other words, most media can be good. It simply takes interest and professional competence—as well as modest financial resources—to be able to carry it off.

PUBLIC OPINION
AND THE PRESS

In general, the press in the United States is operating with a great deal of public support. People have complaints, to be sure. Some don't think the media are always accurate. Others think they are biased in one direction or another. But, for the most part, the public supports the media institutions.

A Gallup poll, summarized in table 8.3, illustrates this quite convincingly. Gallup asked the respondents: "Would you tell me how much respect and confidence you, yourself, have in various institutions?" Included on the list were newspapers and television.

The two media do not fare as well as other institutions, such as organized religion and the schools, or even the U.S. Supreme Court and Congress. But they do quite well overall, with only one in five of those sampled saying they had little or no confidence in the newspaper and television institutions.

Table 8.3 Confidence Ratings of Key U.S. Institutions*

	Percent with Great Deal or Quite a Lot of Confidence	Percent with Some Confidence	Percent with Very Little or No Confidence	Percent with No Opinion
Church or Organized Religion	66	21	11	2
Public Schools	58	27	11	4
U.S. Supreme Court	44	28	17	11
Congress	42	36	14	8
Newspapers	39	39	19	3
Television	38	39	22	2
Labor Unions	30	36	24	10
Big Business	26	36	30	8

* Adapted from *The Gallup Opinion Index*, 97 (July 1973), 10–17. Reprinted by permission.

The critics, of course, may serve as checks on the media. When this group becomes too large, the media may not be able to function properly. At present, however, there is little evidence the critics are a large enough group to hamper the media in their daily newsgathering activities. Rather, the amount of strong support—almost 40 percent in the case of both institutions—should serve as an impetus for the media. Clearly, the press operates in a social system where it has considerable support from public opinion.

CONCLUSIONS

The media are indeed products of the society in which they operate. Their roles have been determined by historical factors and are maintained by present day societal influences. Sometimes these constraints are written into law, and sometimes they are the result of the economic system. Constraints result from the media situation in the community the press system serves as well as from other characteristics of that community. The constraints also result from the organizational behavior of the institution itself.

But the media serve the society. As a functional part of society, they help to shape it. They affect its members and the social fabric.

9
The Effects
of Mass
Communication

Three major sets of barriers and constraints limit the effectiveness of mass communication. Potential *audiences* pose numerous barriers to mass media messages. These messages may be the best creative and intellectual effort of journalism, reproduced and distributed by the most sophisticated of communication technologies available. But many of these messages receive little or no attention from any audience. And even when attended to, numerous psychological and sociological factors influence exactly who pays attention and how they react.

A second locus of constraints is found within the *news media* themselves. Journalism is a professional subculture organized into a series of complementary, yet competing, bureaucracies. In any profession, individual values and attitudes play a significant role in shaping the services and products made available to the public. But because a profession is also a subculture with norms and traditions, the activities considered appropriate (and, in the case of journalism, the stories considered newsworthy) are highly similar from one newsroom to another. To a considerable degree this consensus is dictated by the bureaucratic organization of news media. To get out the daily news quickly, there must be a well-established routine.

Finally, the *society* in which each newspaper and broadcast station seeks its audience imposes constraints. Each society's attitudes, values, and expectations—whether expressed in beliefs, patterns of behavior, or actual laws—shape the mass communication product. And within any society there are differences as well. Los Angeles is *not* San Francisco, and the mass media of the two California cities reflect those cultural differences. Nor is either exactly like Peoria, Dubuque, Syracuse, or any of the hundreds of other communities where local news media produce the daily news. If local mass communication does not reasonably mesh with the local culture, it has no audience and vanishes, victim of the economic constraints on mass media in our society. In extreme cases, failure to meet community standards may bring legal sanctions. Each newspaper, radio station, television station, and cable system must be attuned to its community in order to be an effective communicator and, even more basically, in order to survive.

In short, the practical journalist must thoroughly understand the constraints and potential barriers along the mass communication path. Those who do will be successful communicators. Successful communication occurs when a journalist has assembled and transmitted a message that accurately reflects the real world phenomenon it is based on *and* when audience members receive and understand the contents of the message. Viewed another way, successful messages are those that have an effect—that have made some kind of change in the audience's orientation or response to the environment.

But it isn't necessary for a message to actually reflect reality to have some effect on audience members. In fact, a message that produced some of the most dramatic consequences in the history of broadcasting was fiction, although many people receiving the message didn't realize it at the time.

AN INVASION FROM MARS

On Halloween evening in 1938, the Columbia Broadcasting System performed a freely adapted version of H. G. Wells's novel *War of the Worlds*. Narrated by Orson Welles, the radio play depicted an invasion of Earth by creatures from the planet Mars. Welles and his cast of actors thought the script an appropriate radio drama for the Halloween season, overlooking the larger historical setting of that 1938 Halloween broadcast—continuing traces of the decade-long Great Depression and the first traces of an impending war in Europe.

The performance began innocently enough. Welles set the scene for a piece of fiction that was to focus on modern times and deal with creatures from "across an immense ethereal gulf." These creatures, he said, "regarded this Earth with envious eyes and slowly and surely drew their plans against us."

Then the radio play began with a simulation of a typical dance music show. Then a new voice suddenly said, "Ladies and gentlemen, we interrupt our program of dance music to bring you a special bulletin from the Intercontinental Radio News."

The estimated six million persons listening to the drama on radios in their homes were told, via these fabricated news interruptions, that the Earth was being invaded by Martians. The news included an interview with a scientist who saw something strange in his observations of the atmosphere and a conversation with a farmer who claimed to have actually seen one of the strange visitors. It was, of course, science fiction, with more than a trace of tongue-in-cheek humor.

But of those estimated six million listeners, approximately one million didn't think the whole episode so humorous. In fact, they were extremely frightened or disturbed and did not understand the account was fiction. For them, the Earth was indeed being invaded by persons from another planet. In some cases, the fear led to panic. Some persons literally fled their homes. Some called friends to warn them. Some who were driving their cars at the time ignored all traffic restrictions, speeding home to be with their loved ones for the impending disaster. It was perhaps the most dramatic reaction ever to broadcast programming.

As this episode illustrates, the effects of mass communications can be quite independent of those intended by the sender. That program was designed as entertainment, and for many audience members that is what it produced. But for others, the message led to panic. It is doubtful the programmers expected that to happen.

Quite often a news message produces both the intended immediate effect—an informed audience—and major subsequent effects. The intended effect may be only the first in a series of consequences resulting from the communication process.

When *Washington Post* reporters Bob Woodward and Carl Bernstein, for example, began to unravel the story behind the June 1972 burglary of Democratic party headquarters in the Watergate complex, they only intended to inform their readers about what was going on. It took awhile, but people eventually did understand what the Watergate burglary was all about. And when they did, it provided the base of public opinion needed to oust the guilty leader. Those initial stories by Woodward and Berstein provided the impetus for a lengthy series of events that led to the resignation of Richard Nixon from the presidency slightly more than two years later.

The Orson Welles broadcast and the Watergate story provide an interesting contrast. While the responses to both were extremely dramatic—earning each a unique niche in the history of mass communication—they were quite different in one major respect. The broadcast had direct and immediate effects. The dramatic Watergate effects were indirect, requiring a lengthy, complex series of events and two years to reach their climax. Tracing the effects of mass communication is far from a simple task.

Before examining the nature of mass communication effects in greater detail, consider some less dramatic examples of the effects that news stories can have. One newspaper's April Fool's Day story about a new underpass opening up a dead-end downtown avenue created an immense traffic jam that took the police hours to clear! A televised speech by the president of the United States can increase his standing in the public opinion polls by several points.

Millions of people, after checking a newspaper or radio weather forecast, decide on their wardrobe for the day accordingly. The daily behaviors of public officials are often determined by the news in the morning paper or television news broadcasts. And millions casually chat with their family and friends about what they see in the day's news.

A CATALOG OF RESPONSES

To gain an overview of the many different effects produced by daily journalism, consider this catalog organized in terms of three different perspectives on responses to the news.

The First Perspective

The first perspective considers the *type* of response made. Some mass communications evoke feelings, or *emotional* reaction. Certainly, the Orson Welles broadcast evoked emotional responses far beyond the wildest expectations of its producer. As a more commonplace example, the principal purpose of the human interest story is to evoke an emotional response—feelings of sorrow, amusement, amazement, or whatever, depending on the subject matter at hand. News stories, too, sometimes evoke feelings, positive or negative opinions and evaluations about things in the daily news. Dozens of books on the role of the press in public opinion deal with the influence of the news media in building consensus for or against alternative solutions to the issues of the day.

An even more basic emotional response to the news is described in William Stephenson's *The Play Theory of Mass Communication*. According to this theory and its supporting empirical evidence, a basic human response to news reading and news viewing is enjoyment. Perusing the daily news is a form of intellectual play. This play or enjoyment is just one of many uses and gratifications of the news media examined by scholars of mass communication.

Most of the messages produced by journalists have a quite different purpose. Usually the intended purpose of a news story is to inform. The quiet "I didn't know that!" or "I see" murmured by a reader or viewer in response to a news story is an *intellectual* response differing greatly from the various emotional responses just described. William Randolph Hearst, Joseph Pulitzer and other yellow journalism merchants, as well as more recent purveyors of happy talk TV news shows and supermarket tabloids, have been acutely aware of this distinction between emotional and intellectual responses.

Popular, and even scholarly, attention has more often emphasized emotional rather than intellectual responses to mass communication. But people do learn from the mass media. Numerous studies of both the original Kennedy-

Nixon and more recent Carter-Ford debates demonstrated the tremendous amount and variety of learning among the audiences of these televised series. Less dramatically, George Gerbner's ongoing studies of popular television programming and Alex Edelstein's studies of the general public's knowledge of major issues and problems document the key role of the mass media in the continuing education of our adult populations.

Among children there is also a great variety of learning from mass communication. One television network produces news shorts for children on Saturday morning. A sociological study by the DeFleurs found television programming a major source of information for children about adult occupations. Ward, Wackman and Wartella in *How Children Learn To Buy*, show that children learn a great deal from the advertising content of the mass media.

Scholars are increasingly interested in the role that mass communication plays in the socialization of children. For example, Schramm, Lyle, and Parker's *Television in the Lives of Our Children* documented that children with heavy television exposure entered grade school with superior vocabularies. This kind of incidental learning from mass communication, as well as direct, purposive learning from the news, documentaries, and non-fiction books and magazine articles, continues on through life. Journalism is the major information supplier in our society.

Recent research indicates that the news media are especially adept at creating widespread awareness of a new idea or topic. As Bernard Cohen remarked in *The Press and Foreign Policy,* the press may not tell us what to think, but it is stunningly successful in telling us what to think *about*. Termed the *agenda-setting influence of the press,* this perspective on mass communication effects underscores the role of the press in determining which issues, events, and persons gain our attention.

Not only do the news media bring these issues, events, and persons to public attention, but also the priorities of the press, indexed by its day-by-day patterns of selection and display of the news, become over time the priorities of the public. Each day the media gatekeepers decide which news to carry and how much prominence to give each item. As an inevitable byproduct of this selection process in the normal flow of news, audiences receive cues about the relative importance of these issues, persons, and events and, most importantly, audiences incorporate them into their own personal agendas of the day's concerns.

Both types of reactions discussed so far—emotional and intellectual—are typically covert and hidden from direct observation. Even the most unobtrusive observation of someone reading a newspaper or viewing the news on television is unlikely to yield much information about the actual psychological reaction to each news item. Occasionally, a facial expression or exclamation may indicate some feeling, but for the most part, the daily news is absorbed with little immediate manifest behavior.

On rare occasions it is possible to document a *behavioral* response to the news. The Orson Welles broadcast produced such an occasion. People fled their homes in panic! But for the most part, attempts to link exposure to the news with dramatic behavioral responses, such as turning out to vote on Election Day or participating in an urban riot, have failed because behavioral responses to a news story are seldom immediate or direct.

A news story can provoke feelings. It can make people aware of something. It can on occasion also lead to an immediate decision. But usually some time passes before that decision is translated into any overt behavior. And many other factors, ranging from degree of personal commitment to environmental obstacles, can prevent any translation into actual observable behavior.

In the realm of advertising—another genre of mass communication—a purchase is the ultimate behavior typically desired. But it is a well established fact that advertising messages are only one of several dozen factors determining whether any purchase is actually made.

So while three types of response can be distinguished—emotional, intellectual, and behavioral responses—there is considerably more scientific evidence in hand about the first two than the third.

A Second Perspective

Reactions to mass communication can be considered from a second perspective as well. These effects can be described as either *short-term* or *long-term*. Examples of immediate responses have already been cited. But responses to the day's news, whether emotional, intellectual, or behavioral, can also develop over long periods of time. Wilbur Schramm has analyzed a number of reactions to mass communications in terms of his theory of immediate versus delayed reward. Voters' awareness of and attitudes toward political issues and candidates typically develop over a period of many months. Each day's news is one tiny input. This is a major point made by the research on the agenda-setting influence of the press. This emphasis on long-term, ongoing effects is also key in studies of mass communication and the socialization of children.

Early efforts at tracing the effects of mass communication concentrated on direct and immediate outcomes. We now know that the task is far more complex, that many different kinds of effects extending over many different spans of time—most involving weeks, if not years, to reach threshold—must be delineated.

Part of the continuing controversy about the effects on children of televised violence stems from ambiguities in the empirical evidence about what types of responses are made over what periods of time. Are we concerned with what happens immediately in front of the television set? Or with what happens hours, days, and weeks later on the playground? Or with the more subtle changes in personality that appear in later years? To ask, or attempt to answer, how television has affected the children of the last three decades is to pursue a complex series of paths spanning the lifetime of entire generations.

The Third Perspective

The final perspective used to organize our catalog distinguishes between effects on a single *individual* and effects on an entire *society*. In all the examples cited so far, the response of a single individual has been described, or the response of one person has been compared to the response of another person. But mass communication effects can also be studied at the community and national level.

There is, for example, a vast literature on the role of mass communication in the modernization and industrialization of nations. These studies examine the effects of mass communication on the literacy, urbanization, social attitudes, and cultural practices of villages, towns, and nations, often by comparing populations before and after the introduction of mass communication. The emphasis is on the pattern of societal, rather than individual, response to mass communication.

But one does not have to go to developing nations or rapidly changing communities to find significant social impact by mass communications. Numerous commentators have noted the major changes in the nature of American political campaigns and the national party conventions since the advent of television. Since in modern societies, especially, the mass media are a key part of the culture, the emergence of new media institutions—such as television in the 1940s and 1950s and cable systems and computerized storage and retrieval systems for all kinds of information and entertainment in the 1970s—redefines the very nature of our culture.

At the cultural level, the introduction of television in the 1940s and 1950s stimulated non-fiction library circulation. Through the focusing of attention, mass communication can have profound social effects. Creation of awareness and major influence on the salience of issues, personalities, and topics of all sorts are simply the first stage in the process of social change. Sustained communication over long periods of time can change the very nature of a society and its cultural fabric. Long-term cognitive impact, both on individuals and entire societies, is a domain of major mass communication effects.

ORGANIZING A CATALOG

In table 9.1 we see that the combination of these three perspectives on mass communication effects yields twelve distinct kinds of effects. For each type a representative book title has been listed to illustrate the kinds of empirical knowledge we have on these various outcomes of mass communication. While

Table 9.1 A Selected Bibliography Illustrating Types of Mass Communication Effects

	Individual Effects		
	Emotional	*Intellectual*	*Behavioral*
Short-term	1. Carl Hovland, Irving Janis and Harold Kelley, *Communication and Persuasion* (New Haven, Conn.: Yale University Press, 1953).	2. Donald Shaw and Maxwell McCombs, *The Emergence of American Political Issues: The Agenda-Setting Function of the Press* (St. Paul, Minn.: West Publishing Co., 1977).	3. Hadley Cantril, Hazel Gaudet, and Herta Hertzog, *The Invasion from Mars* (Princeton, N.J.: Princeton University Press, 1940).
Long-term	4. Kurt Lang and Gladys Engel Lang, *Politics and Television* (Chicago, Ill.: Quadrangle Books, 1968).	5. Alex Edelstein, *The Uses of Communication in Decision-Making* (New York: Praeger Publishers, 1974).	6. George Comstock et al., *Television and Human Behavior* (New York: Columbia University Press, 1978).

	Social Effects		
	Emotional	*Intellectual*	*Behavioral*
Short-term	7. Bradley Greenberg and Edwin Parker, *The Kennedy Assassination and the American Public: Social Communication in Crisis* (Stanford, Calif.: Stanford University Press, 1965).	8. Sidney Kraus, *The Great Debates* (Bloomington: Indiana University Press, 1962).	9. Scott Ward, Daniel Wackman, and Ellen Wartella, *How Children Learn To Buy* (Beverly Hills, Calif.: Sage Publications, 1977).
Long-term	10. Sidney Kraus and Dennis Davis, *The Effects of Mass Communication on Political Behavior* (University Park: Pennsylvania State University Press 1976).	11. Wilbur Schramm and Daniel Lerner, eds., *Communication and Change* (Honolulu, Hawaii: East-West Center Press, 1976).	12. Harold Mendelsohn and Irving Crespi, *Polls, Television and the New Politics* (Scranton, Pa.: Chandler, 1970).

a dozen kinds of effects can be distinguished conceptually and illustrated empirically, extensive empirical investigations of mass media effects have concentrated on less than half of these categories.

An exceedingly large number of the studies on mass communication effects belong in category 1 of the catalog. Here, for example, fall most of the attitude change studies that dominated communication research in the 1940s and 1950s. Classical experiments by psychologist Carl Hovland and his colleagues at Yale examined the effects of messages differing in terms of the credibility of the communicator, types of arguments used, and other message variables. The criterion for effects was usually attitude change. Researchers ever since have been concerned with the effects of communication messages on the attitudes of audience members. Only recently have other categories of effects received more research attention.

Why this disproportionate attention to one particular kind of short-term, emotional effect of mass communication? Historically it can be explained by the following three circumstances:

1. At the time questions about the effects of mass communication first gained prominence on the social science research agenda, the concepts of attitude and opinion and reliable research techniques for assessing attitude and opinion were well established in social science. It is hardly surprising that the prominent techniques and concepts of the day were applied to the new questions being asked about the mass media.
2. A substantial body of empirical laboratory and field research produced by Hovland and his associates in the early, formative days of communication research documented the ability of communications to achieve attitude change.
3. Almost at the very moment in the history of communication research that the Yale attitude studies began to wane, major new theories of attitude change and communication appeared in the social sciences. The common idea in these new theories that appeared in the mid-1950s was that attitude change and use of communications were key in resolving conflicts or discrepancies among beliefs and perceptions. These homeostatic theories, some of the most exciting that social science has ever produced, identified and guided the testing of dozens of new hypotheses for more than a decade.

One can view the history of research on mass communication effects as a long-standing fascination with short-term attitudinal effects that only recently has begun to shift toward intellectual, cognitive effects of longer duration. Category 1 in table 9.1 is where the greater portion of the empirical research literature from the 1940s, 1950s, and 1960s falls. And within that category most of the research examines attitudes and opinions.

Considering this distribution of scientific attention, it is not surprising that discussion of attitudes is so prominent in any review of the barriers to effective communication. Selective exposure, selective perception, and selective recall are often the consequences of attitudes held by audience members Professional attitudes as well as personal attitudes also influence the performance of journalists and other professional communicators.

None of this is to say that empirical research has not considered other concepts and other questions about mass communication effects. There is some empirical literature for all the categories in table 9.1. In recent years considerable research has examined effects falling in categories 2, 5, and 8. These categories include informational types of communication effects. The impact of information campaigns and televised instruction, as well as incidental learning from mass communication, have been documented.

MEDIA-AUDIENCE TRANSACTIONS

People use the media. They read the newspaper and magazines. In many homes the television set is on almost constantly. Radio is everywhere. Each day in myriad social settings there are millions of individual transactions between the mass media and the persons in the audiences.

Mass communication is attractive to these audiences. It can literally captivate millions, and as we have seen, this captivation can lead to a variety of social and individual effects. As every advertiser knows, the first step toward influence is to gain attention, to hold an audience long enough for the message to be received and understood. But audiences can raise many barriers to mass communication. Numerous psychological and sociological characteristics of individuals and their social setting affect whether any transaction between the individual and a particular mass communication message is consummated. Occasionally, mass communication has effects because of its sheer ubiquity. But for news and other serious, detailed mass communication messages, a bargain has to be struck between buyer and seller.

This transactional process between communicators and their audiences can be illustrated with what we know about the agenda-setting influence of the news media. The *concept* of agenda-setting and its supporting empirical evidence describes a process in which the mass media exert considerable influence on an individual's perceptions of what are the important topics of the day. But the *theory* of agenda-setting influence developed to date—a map of the agenda-setting concept and its antecedents and consequences—clearly indicates that this influence is far from universal.

Numerous individual characteristics and variations in the social setting in which each person sees and reflects upon the day's news mediate the extent of the agenda-setting influence of the press. Some variables, such as an individual's perceived level of understanding about the day's political issues, enhance the agenda-setting influence of the press. The greater the perceived need for understanding, the greater the influence of the press. On the other hand, some situational variables, such as how frequently a person discusses political issues with others, inhibit the agenda-setting influence of the press. The greater the amount of discussion, the less the influence of the press in defining the important issues of the day.

Production of news messages is the prime concern of editors and reporters. But unless that production process takes the intended consumer into account, it is all in vain. Mass communication succeeds or fails according to how well it is attuned to the intended audience.

CONCLUSION

10
Using Communication Theory

"Journalism is a Career That's Hit Its Heyday," according to a headline in the April 1977 issue of *Money* magazine. "The prestige and benefits of journalism have multiplied—and so has the number of job applicants," the subhead continued.

How long the heyday will last, and its eventual consequences for the profession, were not guessed at in the article. One thing was clear. The journalism profession of the late 1970s is different in many respects from earlier decades. Getting into the profession has become more difficult. As a consequence, those who make it are better trained, at least in the formal sense, than ever before.

What do well-trained journalists look like? And what can students interested in pursuing a career in journalism do to better prepare themselves for the communication tasks to be faced in the future?

Future journalists, to be sure, must be able to gather the information that serves as the raw materials of news copy. Tomorrow's reporters must understand how government works, how decisions are made, how individuals are affected by society. They must have learned how to observe accurately what goes on in the social environment. They must have the perspective to interpret the day's events. They must be sensitive to the implications of those events for their audience.

Future journalists also must be able to write well. Reporting is the process of gathering the raw materials of news. Writing is the process of putting those materials into messages for an audience. The message is the product of the mass communication enterprises. In writing, as well as reporting, then, journalists must be sensitive to the audience. Journalists can only justify their activities in those terms. They are gathering information and writing stories to send to audience members.

But journalists also should be sensitive to the social environment in which they operate. Neither reporting nor writing is done in a vacuum. Rather, reporters and writers are swayed by their colleagues, their superiors, the sources who help them gather the raw materials of news. The journalists of the future should understand this professional environment, for it determines much of what they do.

Finally, the journalists of the future should be aware of the social implications of the mass communication process. The news institutions in society—our newspapers, wire services, television networks, and other news agencies—are the products of historical developments that continue even today to have impact on the news operation. The news gathering and disseminating organizations are influenced as well by other institutions.

For society, information transmittal is a crucial activity. It provides the groundwork for evaluating the effects of mass communications for the individual as well as the society. Journalists who are unaware of or insensitive to the mass communication process and its effects will not be very strong participants in the process.

But these characteristics of the competent journalists of the future—a sensitivity to the audience, an understanding of the social environment in which journalists work, a working knowledge of the societal implications of mass communication—need to be held together somehow. The journalists of the future, in other words, need theory.

The authors of this text would be glad to tell their readers they had just such a theory or a set of theories handy and ready for dissemination. But they don't. Theory building in the field of journalism and mass communication—as well as in much of the social sciences—is only in its infancy. There simply isn't much that even goes by the name of theory, and less that should.

Theories of communications would spell out all the relevant factors that influence human or institutional behavior, tell how all the factors are interrelated, and explain why those relationships hold. In other words, theories would tell journalists what to expect in the future. Theory would identify which messages are most likely to be received, and explain why.

They would tell what kind of newsrooms are best for sound journalistic practice, and why. And they would tell publishers and general managers just what to expect the next time the federal government attempts—if ever it does again—to halt prior publication of a story. That's what good theory would do.

Lacking such integrated theory, the authors have attempted to provide journalists with the raw materials of theory. We have created a catalog of elements for sensitive journalists to keep in mind the next time they produce a communication message. We've tried to spell out the diverse audience reactions to messages, the myriad factors influencing journalistic practice in the news-room and in the field, the underpinnings of the social forces that determine how mass communication is practiced.

Such a compendium, the authors hope, serves several useful purposes. For example, it indicates that the research of the last forty years has indeed provided much useful information. Now, however, it's time to work more at integration—at fashioning the materials in a way to provide insight for the future. It's time to get on with the business of theory building.

More to the point here, however, such a compendium of factors influencing journalistic practice should serve to sensitize future journalists to the task before them. It should make journalists aware of the barriers to successful communications.

That such barriers exist, of course, has been the central theme of this text. The audience members, because of the problems of language, because of difficulties of perception, because of the orientations they have to the message, and because of the social environment in which they receive the communications, erect barriers. These barriers make information transmittal difficult.

The journalist also operates in a social setting, and that setting determines to a large degree what is communicated. So do the background and training of the journalist to the task before him or her. This social setting of the journalist and the orientations he or she brings to communication erect barriers as well.

Finally, the society in which the communication takes place restricts the flow of information and adds yet another layer of restrictions.

Our compendium of barriers has emphasized the negative side of the communication picture. Often, some important pieces of information do not get communicated. A study of registered voters conducted in Syracuse, New York, during the 1976 campaign, for example, showed that even after the vice presidential debate between Republican Robert Dole and Democrat Walter Mondale, many people didn't know much about the two men. Thirty-eight percent of those surveyed could not describe Dole, discuss his background, or give his stands on the issues. For Mondale, the comparable figure was 40 percent. Both men were incumbent U.S. senators at the time.

Much information, however, is successfully communicated by the media. Sixty-two percent *could* describe Dole and 60 percent *could* describe Mondale in the post-debate survey. This information almost certainly came from the media—either directly or indirectly. People who reported watching the vice presidential debate were more likely to be able to describe the candidates than nonviewers. But the fact remains many viewers and nonviewers alike didn't know much about men running for the second highest office of the land. Even among registered voters, the communication was incomplete.

We've attempted to lay the groundwork for an unusual type of communication theory here. Most often in the past, theory has been viewed from the perspective of the audience members, or the recipients of the communication message. We've attempted to view theory from the perspective of the communicator. Audience members, of course, have little direct control over how mass communication is practiced. They can erect barriers against unwanted communications, but they have few other means of controlling the information itself. Journalists, on the other hand, have much to do with the day-to-day activities of mass communications. If journalists come to understand that process—its potentials and its limitations—they will be better able to prepare the messages of mass communication. Journalists can overcome the barriers to communication.

Bibliography

CHAPTER 1

SCHRAMM, WILBUR, "The Nature of Communication Between Humans," in *The Process and Effects of Mass Communication* (rev. ed.), ed. Wilbur Schramm and Donald Roberts, pp. 1–53. Urbana: University of Illinois Press, 1971.

CHAPTER 2

Language

BROWN, ROGER, *Words and Things*. Glencoe, Ill.: The Free Press, 1958.

CARROLL, JOHN B., *Language and Thought*. Englewood Cliffs, N.J.: Prentice-Hall, Inc., 1964.

HERTZLER, JOYCE O., *A Sociology of Language*. New York: Random House, 1965.

Verbal Behavior

MILLER, GEORGE, *Language and Communication*. New York: McGraw-Hill, 1951.

Readability

FLESCH, RUDOLF, "A New Readability Yardstick," *Journal of Applied Psychology*, 32 (1948), 221–33.

KLARE, GEORGE, AND BYRON BUCK, *Know Your Reader: The Scientific Approach to Readability*. New York: Hermitage House, 1954.

TAYLOR, W. L., "'Cloze Procedure': A New Tool for Measuring Readability," *Journalism Quarterly*, 30 (1953), 415–33.

Feeling and Emotion

MERRILL, JOHN, "How *Time* Stereotyped Three U.S. Presidents," *Journalism Quarterly*, 42 (1965), 563–70.

Words and Experience

HENLE, PAUL, ed, *Language, Thought, and Culture*. Ann Arbor: University of Michigan Press, 1958.

WHORF, BENJAMIN, *Language, Thought, and Reality*. Cambridge, Mass.: M.I.T. Press, 1956.

CHAPTER 3

Selecting from Reality

LIPPMANN, WALTER, *Public Opinion*. New York: Macmillan, 1922.

McCOMBS, MAXWELL, AND JOHN M. SMITH, "Perceptual Selection and Communication," *Journalism Quarterly*, 46 (1969), 352–55.

Previous Learning and Experience

ALLPORT, GORDON, AND L. J. POSTMAN, "The Basic Psychology of Rumor," in *Readings in Social Psychology* (3rd ed.), ed. E. E. Maccoby, T. M. Newcomb, and E. L. Hartley. New York: Holt, 1958.

TAGIURI, RENATO, AND LUIGI PETRULLO, eds., *Person Perception and Interpersonal Behavior*. Stanford, Calif.: Stanford University Press, 1958.

Selective Perception

COOPER, EUNICE, AND MARIE JAHODA, "The Evasion of Propaganda: How Prejudiced People Respond to Anti-Prejudice Propaganda," *Journal of Psychology*, 23 (1947), 15–25.

FESTINGER, LEON, *A Theory of Cognitive Dissonance*. Stanford, Calif.: Stanford University Press, 1957.

HASTORF, ALBERT, AND HADLEY CANTRIL, "They Saw a Game: A Case Study," *Journal of Abnormal and Social Psychology*, 49 (1954), 129–34.

Selective Retention

BARTLETT, FREDERICK C., *Remembering*. Cambridge, England: Cambridge University Press, 1932.

LEVINE, J. M., AND GARDNER MURPHY, "The Learning and Forgetting of Controversial Material," *Journal of Abnormal and Social Psychology*, 38 (1943), 507–17.

Perception Process

BROADBENT, DONALD, *Perception and Communication*. London: Pergamon Press, 1958.

CHAPTER 4

BAUER, RAYMOND A., "The Obstinate Audience," *American Psychologist*, 19 (1964), 319–28.

STAR, SHIRLEY A., AND HELEN MACGILL HUGHES, "Report on an Educational Campaign: The Cincinnati Plan for the United Nations," *American Journal of Sociology*, 55 (1950), 389–400.

Selective Exposure

BERELSON, BERNARD R., PAUL F. LAZARSFELD, AND WILLIAM N. MCPHEE, *Voting*. Chicago, Ill.: The University of Chicago Press, 1954.

FESTINGER, LEON, *A Theory of Cognitive Dissonance*. Stanford, Calif.: Stanford University Press, 1957.

FESTINGER, LEON, HENRY W. RIECKEN, JR., AND STANLEY SCHACHTER, *When Prophecy Fails*. Minneapolis: University of Minnesota Press, 1956.

LAZARSFELD, PAUL F., BERNARD F. BERELSON, AND WILLIAM N. MCPHEE, *The People's Choice*. New York: Columbia University Press, 1948.

SEARS, DAVID, AND JONATHAN L. FREEDMAN, "Selective Exposure to Information: A Critical Review," *Public Opinion Quarterly*, 31 (1967), 194–213.

The Chronic "Know-Nothings"

DONOHUE, GEORGE A., PHILLIP J. TICHENOR, AND CLARICE N. OLIEN, "Mass Media and the Knowledge Gap," *Communication Research*, 2 (1975), 3–23.

HYMAN, HERBERT H., AND PAUL B. SHEATSLEY, "Some Reasons Why Information Campaigns Fail," *Public Opinion Quarterly*, 11 (1947), 413–23.

Utility of Information

ATKIN, CHARLES K., "Anticipated Communication and Mass Media Information-Seeking," *Public Opinion Quarterly*, 36 (1972), 188–99.

Personality Factors

WEISS, WALTER, "Effects of the Mass Media of Communication," in *The Handbook of Social Psychology* (vol. 5), ed. Gardner Lindzey and Elliot Aronson, pp. 77–195. Reading, Mass.: Addison-Wesley Publishing Company, 1969.

Uses and Gratifications

BERELSON, BERNARD R., "What 'Missing the Newspaper' Means," in *Communications Research, 1948–1949,* ed. Paul Lazarsfeld and Frank Stanton, pp. 111–29. New York: Harper and Brothers, 1949.

HERTZOG, HERTA, "Motivations and Gratifications of Daily Serial Listeners," in *Radio Research, 1942–43,* ed. Paul Lazarsfeld and Frank Stanton, pp. 3–33. New York: Duell, Sloan and Pearce, 1944.

KATZ, ELIHU, JAY G. BLUMLER, AND MICHAEL GUREVITCH, "Uses of Mass Communication by the Individual," in *Mass Communication Research,* ed. W. Phillips Davison and Frederick T. C. Yu, pp. 11–35. New York: Praeger Publishers, 1974.

The Message Itself

A National Survey of the Content and Readership of the American Newspaper. New York: Newspaper Advertising Bureau, 1972.

CHAPTER 5

Some Involuntary Social Categories

CHAFFEE, STEVEN H., AND DONNA WILSON, "Adult Life Cycle Changes in Mass Media Use." Unpublished paper presented to the Association for Education in Journalism, Ottawa, 1975.

GREENBERG, BRADLEY, AND BRENDA DERVIN, *Use of the Mass Media by the Urban Poor.* New York: Praeger Publishers, 1970.

A National Survey of the Content and Readership of the American Newspaper. New York: Newspaper Advertising Bureau, 1972.

Family Background

CHAFFEE, STEVEN H., JACK M. MCLEOD, AND CHARLES K. ATKIN, "Parental Influences on Adolescent Media Use," *American Behavioral Scientist,* 14 (1971), 323–40.

Interpersonal Environment

BERELSON, BERNARD R., PAUL F. LAZARSFELD, AND WILLIAM N. MCPHEE, *Voting.* Chicago, Ill.: The University of Chicago Press, 1954.

BROWN, ROGER L., AND MICHAEL O'LEARY, "Pop Music in an English Secondary School System," *American Behavioral Scientist,* 14 (1971), 401–13.

DEUTSCHMANN, PAUL J., "Viewing, Conversation, and Voting Intentions," in *The Great Debates,* ed. Sidney Kraus, pp. 232–52. Bloomington: Indiana University Press, 1962.

HARRIS, JACQUELINE, AND MAXWELL MCCOMBS, "The Interpersonal/Mass Communication Interface Among Church Leaders," *Journal of Communication,* 22 (1972), 257–62.

LAZARSFELD, PAUL F., BERNARD R. BERELSON, AND WILLIAM N. MCPHEE, *The People's Choice.* New York: Columbia University Press, 1948.

General

BECKER, LEE B., MAXWELL E. MCCOMBS, AND JACK M. MCLEOD, "The Development of Political Cognitions," in *Political Communication,* ed. Steven H. Chaffee, pp. 21–63. Beverly Hills, Calif.: Sage Publications, 1975.

WEISS, WALTER, "Effects of the Mass Media of Communication," in *The Handbook of Social Psychology* (vol. 5), ed. Gardner Lindzey and Elliot Aronson, pp. 77–195. Reading, Mass.: Addison-Wesley Publishing Company, 1969.

CHAPTER 6

Some Roles
Professional Communicators Play

DOWNIE, LEONARD, *The New Muckrakers.* Washington, D.C.: The New Republic Book Company, 1976.

The Journalist's Baggage

JOHNSTONE, JOHN W. C., EDWARD J. SLAWSKI, AND WILLIAM W. BOWMAN, *The News People: A Sociological Portrait of American Journalists and Their Work.* Urbana: University of Illinois Press, 1976.

THE NATIONAL ADVISORY COMMISSION ON CIVIL DISORDERS, *Report of the Commission.* New York: Bantam, 1968.

Newspeople as Professionals

KIMBALL, PENN, "Journalism: Art, Craft or Profession?" in *The Professions in America,* ed. Kenneth S. Lynn and the editors of *Daedalus,* pp. 243–60. Boston: Houghton Mifflin, 1965.

MCLEOD, JACK M., AND RAMONA R. RUSH, "Professionalization of Latin American and U.S. Journalists," *Journalism Quarterly,* 46 (1969), 583–90.

Newsroom Pressures

BOWERS, DAVID R., "A Report on Activity by Publishers in Directing Newsroom Decisions," *Journalism Quarterly,* 44 (1967), 43–52.

BREED, WARREN, "Social Control in the Newsroom: A Functional Analysis," *Social Forces,* 33 (1955), 326–35.

CROUSE, TIMOTHY, *The Boys on the Bus.* New York: Ballantine, 1973.

SIGELMAN, LEE, "Reporting the News: An Organizational Analysis," *American Journal of Sociology,* 79 (1973), 132–51.

CHAPTER 7

News Definitions

BAGDIKIAN, BEN, *The Information Machines.* New York: Harper and Row, 1971.

DONOHUE, GEORGE A., PHILLIP J. TICHENOR, AND CLARICE N. OLIEN, "Gatekeeping: Mass Media Systems and Information Control," in *Current Perspectives in Mass Communication Research,* ed. F. Gerald Kline and Phillip J. Tichenor, pp. 441–69. Beverly Hills, Calif.: Sage Publications, 1972.

LINDEBORG, RICHARD A., AND GERALD C. STONE, "News Values as Reflected in News Content Found Stable from 1950 to 1970," *ANPA News Research Bulletin,* 7 (1974).

ROSHCO, BERNARD, *Newsmaking.* Chicago, Ill.: University of Chicago Press, 1975.

WHITE, DAVID MANNING, "The 'Gatekeeper': A Case Study in the Selection of News," *Journalism Quarterly,* 27 (1950), 383–90.

Reporter-Source Relations

DREW, DAN G., "Roles and Decision Making of Three Television Beat Reporters," *Journal of Broadcasting,* 16 (1972), 165–73.

GIEBER, WALTER, AND WALTER JOHNSON, "The City Hall 'Beat': A Study of Reporter and Source Roles," *Journalism Quarterly,* 38 (1961), 289–97.

Technological Constraints

BAGDIKIAN, BEN H., "Professional Personnel and Organizational Structure in the Mass Media," in *Mass Communication Research,* ed. W. Phillips Davison and Frederick T. C. Yu, pp. 122–42. New York: Praeger Publishers, 1974.

TUCHMAN, GAYE, "Making News by Doing Work: Routinizing the Unexpected," *American Journal of Sociology,* 79 (1973), 110–31.

The Reporter's Tools

McCOMBS, MAXWELL E., DONALD L. SHAW, AND DAVID GREY, eds., *Handbook of Reporting Methods.* Boston, Mass.: Houghton Mifflin, 1976.

MEYER, PHILLIP, *Precision Journalism.* Bloomington: Indiana University Press, 1973.

CHAPTER 8

The Historical Context

SIEBERT, FRED, THEODORE PETERSON, AND WILBUR SCHRAMM, *Four Theories of the Press*. Urbana: University of Illinois Press, 1956.

Mass Communication

McQUAIL, DENIS, *Communication*. New York: Longman, 1975.

Functions
of Mass Communication

LASSWELL, HAROLD D., "The Structure and Function of Communication in Society," in *The Communication of Ideas,* ed. L. Bryson. New York: Harper and Brothers, 1948.
WRIGHT, CHARLES R., *Mass Communication*. New York: Random House, 1975.

Legal Barriers to Mass Communication

GORA, JOEL M., *The Rights of Reporters*. New York: Discus Books, 1974.
UNGAR, SANFORD J., *The Papers & The Papers*. New York: E. P. Dutton, 1972.

Economic Constraints
on the Press

McCOMBS, MAXWELL E., "Mass Media in the Marketplace," *Journalism Monographs,* 24 (1972).

Influences
of Journalistic Competition

STEMPEL, GUIDO H., III, "Effects on Performance of a Cross-Media Monopoly," *Journalism Monographs,* 29 (1973).

Community Constraints
on the Press

BECKER, LEE B., RANDY BEAM, AND JOHN RUSSIAL, "Correlates of Daily Newspaper Performance in New England," *Journalism Quarterly,* 55 (1978), 100–108.

CHAPTER 9

BERELSON, BERNARD R., PAUL F. LAZARSFELD, AND WILLIAM N. McPHEE, *Voting*. Chicago, Ill.: University of Chicago Press, 1954.

BLUMLER, JAY G., AND DENIS MCQUAIL, *Television in Politics*. Chicago, Ill.: University of Chicago Press, 1969.

CANTRIL, HADLEY, HAZEL GAUDET, AND HERTA HERTZOG, *The Invasion from Mars*. Princeton, N.J.: Princeton University Press, 1940.

COHEN, BERNARD, *The Press and Foreign Policy*. Princeton, N.J.: Princeton University Press, 1963.

COMSTOCK, GEORGE, STEVEN CHAFFEE, NATAN KATZMAN, MAXWELL MCCOMBS, AND DONALD ROBERTS, *Television and Human Behavior*. New York: Columbia University Press, 1978.

DEFLEUR, MELVIN L., AND SANDRA BALL-ROKEACH, *Theories of Mass Communication* (3rd ed.). New York: David McKay, 1975.

EDELSTEIN, ALEX, *The Uses of Communication in Decision-Making*. New York: Praeger Publishers, 1974.

FESTINGER, LEON, *A Theory of Cognitive Dissonance*. Stanford, Calif.: Stanford University Press, 1957.

GREENBERG, BRADLEY, AND EDWIN PARKER, *The Kennedy Assassination and the American Public: Social Communication in Crisis*. Stanford, Calif.: Stanford University Press, 1965.

HOVLAND, CARL, IRVING JANIS, AND HAROLD KELLEY, *Communication and Persuasion*. New Haven, Conn.: Yale University Press, 1953.

KLAPPER, JOSEPH, *The Effects of Mass Communication*. New York: Free Press, 1960.

KRAUS, SIDNEY, ed., *The Great Debates*. Bloomington: Indiana University Press, 1962.

KRAUS, SIDNEY, AND DENNIS DAVIS, *The Effects of Mass Communication on Political Behavior*. University Park: Pennsylvania State University Press, 1976.

LANG, KURT, AND GLADYS E. LANG, *Politics and Television*. Chicago, Ill.: Quadrangle Books, 1968.

LAZARSFELD, PAUL F., BERNARD BERELSON, AND HAZEL GAUDET, *The People's Choice*. New York: Columbia University Press, 1944.

LERBINGER, OTTO, *Designs for Persuasive Communication*. Englewood Cliffs, N.J.: Prentice-Hall, Inc., 1972.

LIPPMANN, WALTER, *Public Opinion*. New York: Macmillan, 1922.

MENDELSOHN, HAROLD, AND IRVING CRESPI, *Polls, Television and the New Politics*. Scranton, Pa.: Chandler, 1970.

PATTERSON, THOMAS E., AND ROBERT D. MCCLURE, *The Unseeing Eye*. New York: G.P. Putnam's Sons, 1976.

SCHRAMM, WILBUR, AND DANIEL LERNER, eds., *Communication and Change*. Honolulu, Hawaii: East-West Center Press, 1976.

SCHRAMM, WILBUR, JACK LYLE, AND EDWIN PARKER, *Television in the Lives of Our Children*. Stanford, Calif.: Stanford University Press, 1961.

SCHRAMM, WILBUR, AND DONALD ROBERTS, *The Process and Effects of Mass Communication*. Urbana: University of Illinois Press, 1971.

SHAW, DONALD L., AND MAXWELL MCCOMBS, eds., *The Emergence of American Political Issues*. St. Paul, Minn.: West Publishing Co., 1977.

WARD, SCOTT, DANIEL WACKMAN, AND ELLEN WARTELLA, *How Children Learn to Buy*. Beverly Hills, Calif.: Sage Publications, 1977.

Index